Apostolic Principles

A Guide for Beginners

Apostolic Principles

A Guide for Beginners

Michael E. Crocker

NewStart Press
2014

First Printing: 2014

ISBN 978-1-312-30349-2

NewStart Press
201B W. Butler Road, #121
Greenville, SC 29607

www.newstartpress.com

Ordering Information:

Special discounts are available on quantity purchases by corporations, associations, educators, and others. For details, contact the publisher at the above listed address.

U.S. trade bookstores and wholesalers:

Please contact NewStart Press

Tel: (864) 248-6500
Email info@newstartpress.com

Contents

Introduction

Your first visit to an Apostolic Pentecostal church will undoubtedly be a unique experience for you. You may find it very different from other church services you have attended, and may not know just how to react to the informal worship and structure. The purpose of this book is to answer any questions you may have about Apostolic doctrines or worship styles. As you read this book you will discover that Apostolic practices are solidly rooted in the Bible, though much of what you see may appear to be very informal and relaxed on the surface.

What do the terms "Apostolic" and "Pentecostal" mean?

The term "Apostolic" means "like the Apostles." Apostolic churches believe strongly in following the teachings of the original apostles (specifically, the disciples of Jesus and Paul). Since the time of the Apostles, many traditions and doctrines that have no biblical basis have found their way into the church. Apostolic Pentecostals seek to be as faithful as possible to what the original apostles taught. While we respect church traditions and creeds, on matters of doctrine we appeal solely to scripture.

What the apostles preached to sinners is recorded in the book called the Acts of the Apostles in the New Testament. While the other books of the Bible are equally inspired of God and are useful for teaching Christians how to live, it is only in the Book of Acts that we find a historical account of when, where, and how the apostles preached to sinners. The seriousness of carefully following the preaching of the apostles is found in the words of the apostle Paul:

> ***Galatians 1:8-9*** [8] *But though we, or an angel from heaven, preach any other gospel unto you than that which we* [the apostles] *have preached unto you, let him be accursed.* [9] *As we said before, so say I now again, If any man preach any other gospel unto you than that ye have received, let him be accursed.*

The word "Pentecostal," on the other hand, comes from the fact that Pentecostal churches trace their roots to the outpouring of the Holy Spirit on the day of Pentecost, as described in the second chapter of Acts. On that day, the one hundred and twenty disciples of Jesus were filled with the Holy Spirit and spoke with other tongues through the power of the Holy Spirit. By definition, a Pentecostal church is one that teaches that the various supernatural gifts of the Spirit, including, but not limited to, speaking in tongues, are still in operation in the church today. Many denominations believe and teach that these gifts died with the apostles, but we respectfully disagree . This will be discussed in much more detail in later chapters. For now, let's move to Chapter One and see if we can answer some questions you may already have.

Chapter 1: Why Do You Worship the Way You Do?

Why do some people raise their hands when they pray?

Believers have lifted their hands toward God in worship for centuries. Raised hands are a symbol of complete surrender, and by raising your hands to God you are submitting, or surrendering, yourself to Him. The practice of raising hands in prayer is not only practiced throughout the Bible, it is encouraged and even commanded. Consider the following examples:

> ***Genesis 14:22*** *...I have lift up mine hand unto the LORD..*

> ***Nehemiah 8:6*** *...And all the people answered, Amen, Amen, with lifting up their hands: and they bowed their heads, and worshiped the LORD with their faces to the ground.*

Bowing the head and putting one's face to the ground were also common forms of worship in Bible times.

> ***Psalm 28:2*** *Hear the voice of my supplications, when I cry unto thee, when I lift up my hands toward thy holy oracle.*

In the preceding verse we see the writer crying unto the Lord in prayer. Praying out loud is a form of worship commonly found in Pentecostal churches.

> ***Psalm 63:4*** *Thus will I bless thee while I live: I will lift up my hands in thy name.*

> ***Psalm 134:2*** *Lift up your hands in the sanctuary* [church], *and bless the LORD.*

> ***Psalm 141:2*** *Let my prayer be set forth before thee as incense; and the lifting up of my hands as the evening sacrifice.*

> ***Lamentations 2:19*** *Arise, cry out in the night: in the beginning of the watches pour out thine heart like water before the face of*

the Lord: lift up thy hands toward him for the life of thy young children, that faint for hunger in the top of every street.

Notice that the writer spoke of "crying out" to God in prayer as well as lifting up hands.

I Timothy 2:8 *I will therefore that men pray every where, lifting up holy hands...*

Hebrews 12:12 *Wherefore lift up the hands which hang down, and the feeble knees;*

What about falling on your face before God?

Ezekiel 11:13 *...Then fell I down upon my face, and cried with a loud voice, and said, Ah Lord GOD! wilt thou make a full end of the remnant of Israel?*

Ezekiel speaks of "a loud voice" in the preceding example in addition to falling on his face in prayer.

Why do some people leap and dance?

The Bible provides numerous examples of dancing before the Lord, and even encourages us to do so:

Exodus 15:20 *And Miriam the prophetess, the sister of Aaron, took a timbrel in her hand; and all the women went out after her with timbrels and with dances.*

II Samuel 6:14 *And David danced before the LORD with all his might...*

II Samuel 6:16 *...saw king David leaping and dancing before the LORD...*

Psalm 30:11 *Thou hast turned for me my mourning into dancing...*

Psalm 149:3 *Let them praise his name in the dance...*

Psalm 150:4 *Praise him with the timbrel* [tambourine] *and dance...*

Ecclesiastes 3:4 *A time to weep, and a time to laugh; a time to mourn, and a time to dance...*

Jeremiah 31:4 *Again I will build thee, and thou shalt be built, O virgin of Israel: thou shalt again be adorned with thy tabrets, and shalt go forth in the dances of them that make merry.*

Jeremiah 31:13 *Then shall the virgin rejoice in the dance, both young men and old together: for I will turn their mourning into joy....*

Luke 6:23 *Rejoice ye in that day, and leap for joy: for, behold, your reward is great in heaven:*

Acts 3:8 *And he leaping up stood, and walked, and entered with them into the temple, walking, and leaping, and praising God.*

Dancing only takes on a negative connotation when God is not the object of the dance. The Bible teaches us that everything should be done decently and in order, so dancing that is physically suggestive or does not glorify God in some way is never proper.

It is clear from the scriptures that leaping and dancing were very much a part of biblical worship, and thus are still practiced in Pentecostal churches today. It is unfortunate that many churches have abandoned these scriptural forms of worship and thereby deny individuals one of the greatest blessings that God can give, that of expressing oneself physically and emotionally in praise to God. Can you imagine going to a football game or political rally and not being allowed to vocalize your feelings, or clap your hands for your favorite team or candidate? Isn’t God so much more deserving of our praise than a sports team or celebrity?

Why does everyone pray out loud? I am used to quiet church services.

Like every other form of worship we have looked at thus far, vocal (audible) prayer has strong biblical support. Consider the following:

> ***I Kings 1:40*** *And all the people came up after him, and the people piped with pipes, and rejoiced with great joy, so that the earth rent with the sound of them.*

The rejoicing was so loud that the earth "rent" (or split) from the sound! A few more examples:

> ***I Chronicles 15:28*** *Thus all Israel brought up the ark of the covenant of the LORD with shouting, and with sound of the cornet, and with trumpets, and with cymbals, making a noise with psalteries and harps.*
>
> ***II Chronicles 15:14*** *And they sware unto the LORD with a loud voice, and with shouting...*
>
> ***II Chronicles 30:21*** *...and the Levites and the priests praised the LORD day by day, singing with loud instruments unto the LORD.*
>
> ***Ezra 3:11*** *...And all the people shouted with a great shout, when they praised the LORD...*
>
> ***Ezra 3:13*** *So that the people could not discern the noise of the shout of joy from the noise of the weeping of the people: for the people shouted with a loud shout, and the noise was heard afar off.*

The noise of the people shouting for joy was heard from a great distance. This is a far cry from the quiet worship of many churches.

> ***Nehemiah 9:4*** *...cried with a loud voice unto the LORD their God.*

> ***Nehemiah 12:42-43*** *...the singers sang loud...43 ...God had made them rejoice with great joy: the wives also and the children rejoiced: so that the joy of Jerusalem was heard even afar off.*

An entire city worshiped so loudly that their praise was heard from afar!

> ***Job 36:29*** *Also can any understand the spreadings of the clouds, or the noise of his tabernacle* [church]*?*

> ***Psalm 5:11*** *...let them ever shout for joy...*

> ***Psalm 32:11*** *...shout for joy...*

> ***Psalm 33:3*** *... play skilfully with a loud noise.*

> ***Psalm 35:27*** *Let them shout for joy, and be glad...*

> ***Psalm 47:1*** *...O clap your hands, all ye people; shout unto God with the voice of triumph.*

Hand clapping is another biblical form of worship, as the preceding verse illustrates.

> ***Psalm 55:17*** *Evening, and morning, and at noon, will I pray, and cry aloud: and he shall hear my voice.*

> ***Psalm 66:1*** *...Make a joyful noise unto God...:*

> ***Psalm 66:8*** *... make the voice of his praise to be heard:*

This last passage is especially interesting because we learn from it that God not only allows vocal praise, but He *commands* it!

> ***Psalm 81:1*** *...Sing aloud unto God our strength: make a joyful noise unto the God of Jacob.*

Psalm 95:1 *...let us make a joyful noise to the rock of our salvation. 2 Let us come before his presence with thanksgiving, and make a joyful noise unto him with psalms.*

Psalm 98:4 *Make a joyful noise unto the LORD, all the earth: make a loud noise, and rejoice, and sing praise.*

Psalm 98:6 *With trumpets and sound of cornet make a joyful noise before the LORD, the King.*

Psalm 100:1 *...Make a joyful noise unto the LORD...*

Psalm 132:9 *...let thy saints shout for joy.*

Psalm 132:16 *...her saints shall shout aloud for joy.*

Psalm 150:5 *Praise him upon the loud cymbals...*

Isaiah 12:6 *Cry out and shout, thou inhabitant of Zion: for great is the Holy One of Israel in the midst of thee.*

Jeremiah 31:7 *...thus saith the LORD; Sing with gladness for Jacob, and shout among the chief of the nations:*

Zephaniah 3:14 *Sing, O daughter of Zion; shout, O Israel; be glad and rejoice with all the heart, O daughter of Jerusalem.*

Zechariah 9:9 *Rejoice greatly, O daughter of Zion; shout, O daughter of Jerusalem...*

Luke 17:15 *...with a loud voice glorified God,*

Luke 19:37 *...the whole multitude of the disciples began to rejoice and praise God with a loud voice...*

Acts 16:25 *And at midnight Paul and Silas prayed, and sang praises unto God: and the prisoners heard them.*

In Acts 2 it is noteworthy that the praise and worship of the 120 disciples of Jesus on the day of Pentecost appeared to some to be the actions of intoxicated individuals:

> ***Acts 2:13*** *Others mocking said, These men are full of new wine.*

Even today, our praise may seem different or even strange to those who are not accustomed to it; however, this is primarily because so many Churches today have drifted away from true, heartfelt, biblical worship.

If you are concerned about feeling pressured to worship in a particular manner, there is no need to be concerned. You will never be pressured to worship in a manner that you are uncomfortable with. We simply encourage you to open up to God and allow Him to commune with you in a way will edify you.

Keep in mind that the Bible teaches us that God dwells in our praise. God is, above all else, holy, and He only responds to sincere, heartfelt worship. If you truly wish to communicate with God, the best approach is through praise and worship.

> ***Psalm 22:3*** *But thou art holy, O thou that inhabitest the praises of Israel.*

The preaching is much more lively and passionate than I am used to. Why is this?

Lively preaching is as biblical as lively praise and worship:

> ***Isaiah 58:1*** *Cry aloud, spare not, lift up thy voice like a trumpet, and show my people their transgression, and the house of Jacob their sins.*

Often when Jesus preached he cried out loudly:

> ***John 7:37*** *In the last day, that great day of the feast, Jesus stood and cried, saying, If any man thirst, let him come unto me, and drink.*

It is difficult for the Pentecostal preacher to imagine being anything but passionate about the sermons he preaches. Subjects like heaven, hell, the crucifixion, and deliverance from sin are subjects that should elicit a passionate response from any believer.

Chapter 2: What Is Repentance?

The first thing the Bible commands a new believer to do is to repent. This chapter explains just what that means, and how repentance relates to believing, baptism, and receiving the Holy Ghost.

I hear a lot of talk about "repenting" and that I need to "repent." What does this mean?

Repentance is simply the act of making a conscious decision to confess your past sins to God, and determining to no longer live a life of sin. It is a conscious decision to turn away from sin and turn to God. It is what many churches refer to as praying the "sinner's prayer."

I believe in God. Isn't that enough? Or do I still have to repent?

Believing alone is not enough, because even the devils believe in God:

> ***James 2:19*** *Thou believest that there is one God; thou doest well: the devils also believe, and tremble.*

Simply believing in the existence of God is not the same as following Him. Many people believe in God without serving Him, and in many cases are very evil in their deeds. Repentance is more than just believing in God; it is the process of changing direction — a decision to live for God and obey His Word to the best of our ability. A person is not saved because he or she believes; a person is saved because he or she truly repents and obeys the Gospel.

Jesus demanded repentance throughout His ministry:

> ***Matthew 4:17*** *From that time Jesus began to preach, and to say, Repent: for the kingdom of heaven is at hand.*

Matthew 9:13 *But go ye and learn what that meaneth, I will have mercy, and not sacrifice: for I am not come to call the righteous, but sinners to repentance.*

Matthew 11:20 *Then began he to upbraid the cities wherein most of his mighty works were done, because they repented not:*

Luke 13:3 *I tell you, Nay: but, except ye repent, ye shall all likewise perish.*

In the preceding verse, Jesus declared that those who fail to repent will perish. Simple faith alone was insufficient.

When Jesus issued what is known as the "Great Commission" to His disciples, He specifically included repentance in what they were to teach:

Luke 24:47 *And that repentance and remission of sins should be preached in his name among all nations, beginning at Jerusalem.*

Jesus' twelve main disciples were called Apostles after He ascended into heaven and they took over the earthly leadership of the Church. They also preached repentance:

Mark 6:12 *And they went out, and preached that men should repent.*

Acts 2:38 *Then Peter said unto them, Repent, and be baptized every one of you in the name of Jesus Christ for the remission of sins, and ye shall receive the gift of the Holy Ghost.*

Acts 3:19 *Repent ye therefore, and be converted, that your sins may be blotted out, when the times of refreshing shall come from the presence of the Lord;*

Acts 17:30 *And the times of this ignorance God winked at; but now commandeth all men every where to repent:*

My life is pretty miserable right now. I really could use a change. Will God hear me?

Yes, but only if your motives for repenting are pure. Many people repent because they feel sorry for themselves and want a "quick fix" to put their lives back in order. Perhaps they are going through financial difficulty or marital discord. Sometimes it is because they are experiencing health problems. They turn to God in their hour of need, and all too often forget Him after the problem is resolved. This "repentance" is not true repentance at all. Look at the next verse:

> ***II Corinthians 7:10*** *For godly sorrow worketh repentance to salvation not to be repented of: but the sorrow of the world worketh death.*

This "sorrow of the world" is deadly because it lends a false sense of security to the sinner. The individual who has been to church, wept at the altar, and felt the presence of God is led to believe that he is "saved." No permanent change in lifestyle occurs, and soon the believer is right back in the same predicament as before, only this time convinced that he is "saved" and all is well. This can even turn some against God completely, since new prayers for deliverance from new problems seem to go unanswered. The real problem, of course, is not God, but the faulty motivation behind the prayers and the desire for a partial solution rather than a permanent change.

I have never really prayed before. What do I have to say?

The exact words are not as important as the attitude of the heart. There is no such thing as a specific "sinner's prayer" in the Bible. Repentance is not so much a prayer as it is a change in attitude. Simply tell God that you are sorry for your past sins, and mean it. Purpose in your heart, that you will live for Him. The Bible promises us that He will hear and honor such a prayer, so you simply have to accept that promise:

> ***Proverbs 28:13*** *He that covereth his sins shall not prosper: but whoso confesseth and forsaketh them shall have mercy.*

> ***1 John 1:9*** *If we confess our sins, he is faithful and just to forgive us our sins, and to cleanse us from all unrighteousness.*

How will I know that I have truly repented? Will God give me some kind of sign that He has heard me?

True repentance will be accompanied by a changed life and a desire to obey God's commands. John the Baptist believed so strongly in repentance that he refused to baptize people who had not produced the "fruit" of repentance:

> ***Luke 3:7-8*** [7] *Then said he to the multitude that came forth to be baptized of him, O generation of vipers, who hath warned you to flee from the wrath to come?* [8] *Bring forth therefore fruits worthy of repentance, and begin not to say within yourselves, We have Abraham to our father: for I say unto you, That God is able of these stones to raise up children unto Abraham.*

In addition, because baptism is a command, a truly repentant sinner will obey the command to be baptized. We will discuss baptism in more detail in the next chapter, but in the meantime, there are some basic principles that will help you on your journey. First, go to every church service you possibly can. The Bible says:

> ***Romans 10:17*** *So then faith cometh by hearing, and hearing by the word of God.*

Since faith comes by hearing, and hearing by the Word of God, you need to hear the Word of God as much as possible. Note that the verse does not mention reading the Word (though this is important as well), but focuses on **hearing** the Word. Something happens in your spirit when you hear the Word. There is no substitute for hearing preaching. The more you hear the Word, the stronger your faith becomes. A quick way to drift away from God is to start missing church services regularly.

Second, worship with all your heart, soul, mind, and strength. The Bible says:

> ***Psalm 22:3*** *But thou art holy, O thou that inhabitest the praises of Israel.*

There is something about our praise that attracts God. The more you worship, the stronger your relationship with God becomes.

Third, pray and read your Bible every day. This doesn't mean you must pray for an hour or read five chapters each day; quality time is more important than quantity. A sincere five-minute prayer is more effective than a stale one-hour prayer. Prayer is nothing more than talking to God like you would a friend.

When reading your Bible, try to read at least a few verses or a chapter every day. The Word of God is quick and powerful (Hebrews 4:12), meaning it does something in and to our spirit when we read it. In addition, God speaks to us from His Word, so we have to allow this to happen by studying it.

I recommend reading from a different part of the Bible each day rather than straight through. The reason for this is that there are parts of the Bible that new converts can find confusing or tedious. There are six major divisions of the Bible:

a. The Pentateuch (the first five books of the Bible, Genesis through Deuteronomy)

b. History (Joshua through Esther)

c. Poetry (Job through Song of Solomon)

d. The Prophets (Isaiah through Malachi)

e. The Gospels and Acts (Matthew through Acts)

f. The Epistles and Revelation (Romans through Revelation)

On Monday, for instance, you could read one chapter from the Pentateuch, on Tuesday you could read one from one of the books on History, on Wednesday one from Poetry, and so on. The advantage to this approach is that you do not get "bogged down" in the Law or Prophets for weeks at a time.

Bear in mind that believing and repentance are simply the beginning, not the end, of the process of being "born again." Just as a child is carried nine months in the womb of a mother, the moment we truly believe we are "conceived" and set in motion the birth process through faith. Genuine faith will cause us to repent, to be baptized, and ultimately lead to being filled with the Holy Ghost. This is the birth of "water" and "Spirit" Jesus spoke of in John 3:5.

The Bible commands (it does not recommend or suggest) us to be baptized in the name of Jesus Christ for the remission of sins (this is discussed in the next chapter). When you have truly obeyed God in this manner, you are promised the gift of the Holy Ghost (discussed in chapter four).

Chapter 3: The Whys and Hows of Water Baptism

What is the purpose of baptism?

We all know that Jesus died, was buried, and rose again. This is what we refer to as the "Gospel," or the "good news" of Jesus Christ.

Many people are surprised to learn that we are commanded by the Bible to obey (not just believe) the Gospel:

> ***Romans 10:16*** *But they have not all obeyed the gospel. For Esaias saith, Lord, who hath believed our report?*
>
> ***II Thessalonians 1:8*** *In flaming fire taking vengeance on them that know not God, and that obey not the gospel of our Lord Jesus Christ:*
>
> ***I Peter 4:17*** *For the time is come that judgment must begin at the house of God: and if it first begin at us, what shall the end be of them that obey not the gospel of God?*

True faith will compel us to obey, rather than merely believe, the Gospel. If you recall from the previous chapter, even the devils believe; believing alone is not the same as obeying the gospel.

If the Gospel is the death, burial, and resurrection of Jesus Christ, how do we obey it? There are three fundamental steps in obedience to the Gospel, just as there are three phases (death, burial, and resurrection) in the Gospel of Jesus Christ. These three steps are:

1. Repentance. Through repentance our old nature dies.

2. Baptism. In baptism our old nature is buried.

3. Receiving the Holy Ghost. When we receive the Holy Ghost, we are "resurrected" as a new person.

Just as Jesus died, was buried, and rose again, we die, are buried, and rise again as well. We have already discussed repentance in the previous chapter, and will discuss the Holy Ghost in the next chapter. This chapter will focus on water baptism.

Is baptism optional, or is it a command?

Consider the following verses:

> ***Mark 16:16*** *He that believeth and is baptized shall be saved; but he that believeth not shall be damned.*
>
> ***John 3:5*** *Jesus answered, Verily, verily, I say unto thee, Except a man be born of water and of the Spirit, he cannot enter into the kingdom of God.*
>
> ***Acts 2:38*** *Then Peter said unto them, Repent, and be baptized every one of you in the name of Jesus Christ for the remission of sins, and ye shall receive the gift of the Holy Ghost.*
>
> ***Acts 10:48*** *And he commanded them to be baptized in the name of the Lord. Then prayed they him to tarry certain days.*
>
> ***Acts 22:16*** *And now why tarriest thou? arise, and be baptized, and wash away thy sins, calling on the name of the Lord.*
>
> ***I Peter 3:21*** *The like figure whereunto even baptism doth also now save us (not the putting away of the filth of the flesh, but the answer of a good conscience toward God,) by the resurrection of Jesus Christ:*
>
> ***Romans 6:4*** *Therefore we are buried with him by baptism into death: that like as Christ was raised up from the dead by the glory of the Father, even so we also should walk in newness of life.*
>
> ***Colossians 2:12*** *Buried with him in baptism, wherein also ye are risen with him through the faith of the operation of God, who hath raised him from the dead.*

Today some suggest that we can ignore the preceding verses and choose not to be baptized. However, it is our position that baptism is a command and part of obedience to the gospel. After dying through repentance, we are buried through baptism. Why not simply obey the commands? How can a person claim to have genuinely repented while simultaneously rejected one of the clearest commands of scripture? Ultimately, we shall be judged by the Word itself:

> ***John 12:48*** *He that rejecteth me, and receiveth not my words, hath one that judgeth him: the word that I have spoken, the same shall judge him in the last day.*

The Word will judge us when we stand before God, and it does not "recommend" or "suggest" baptism. It commands it as part of obedience to the Gospel.

The seriousness and urgency of baptism is illustrated by the fact that new converts in the Bible were immediately baptized, sometimes in the late hours of the night or the wee hours of the morning. In contrast to the practice of many churches, in the Bible there is no waiting for months to be baptized. In the book of Acts there is no delay while the church waits for an annual baptism service to roll around. No, we find that in the apostles always treated baptism with a sense of urgency.

> ***Acts 16:33*** *And he took them the same hour of the night, and washed their stripes; and was baptized, he and all his, straightway.*

Even though Paul and Silas had been beaten bloody, baptism was important enough that they baptized the Philippian jailor and his family immediately upon being miraculously delivered from prison, after midnight! They did not wait days or weeks or months. They baptized this man after midnight, even with their backs bloody from the beating they had received the day before.

Perhaps Paul treated baptism so urgently because Ananias was just as urgent during Paul's own conversion:

Acts 9:18-19 [18] *And immediately there fell from his eyes as it had been scales: and he received sight forthwith, and arose, and was baptized.* [19] *And when he had received meat, he was strengthened.*

What is sometimes overlooked in Paul's conversion is the fact that he had been fasting without food or water for three days prior to receiving his sight, yet was baptized before he ate or drank anything! Most of us, if we had been without food or water for three days, would eat first and worry about baptism later. Not Ananias; baptism was too important. He baptized Paul first.

Is it important how I am baptized? Can I just be sprinkled?

There is no record in the Bible of anyone ever being sprinkled in baptism. The practice of sprinkling in baptism evolved hundreds of years after the apostolic age, and was not part of their teaching. Since we have already seen that baptism typifies burial, it is only logical that one would be submerged in water just as one is completely covered with earth when one is buried. The very word "baptism" means to "submerge, immerse." Everyone in the Bible who was baptized went down into the water:

Matthew 3:16 *And Jesus, when he was baptized, went up straightway out of the water: and, lo, the heavens were opened unto him, and he saw the Spirit of God descending like a dove, and lighting upon him:*

John 3:23 *And John also was baptizing in Aenon near to Salim, because there was much water there: and they came, and were baptized.*

If John was sprinkling baptismal candidates, there would be no need for "much" water.

Acts 8:38 *And he commanded the chariot to stand still: and they went down both into the water, both Philip and the eunuch; and he baptized him.*

Are the words pronounced over a person in baptism important?

Once again, let's look at the Bible record:

> ***Acts 2:38*** *Then Peter said unto them, Repent, and be baptized every one of you in the name of Jesus Christ for the remission of sins, and ye shall receive the gift of the Holy Ghost.*

> ***Acts 4:12*** *Neither is there salvation in any other: for there is none other name under heaven given among men, whereby we must be saved.*

> ***Acts 8:16*** *(For as yet he was fallen upon none of them: only they were baptized in the name of the Lord Jesus.)*

> ***Acts 10:48*** *And he commanded them to be baptized in the name of the Lord. Then prayed they him to tarry certain days.*

> ***Acts 19:5*** *When they heard this, they were baptized in the name of the Lord Jesus.*

We see that the biblical formula was baptism in the name of Jesus. There is no record in the Bible of anyone ever being baptized in the titles Father, Son, and Holy Ghost, as is practiced in most churches today.

Why do so many churches baptize in the name of the Father, Son, and Holy Ghost, if this was never done in the Bible?

The practice of baptizing in the name of the Father, Son, and Holy Ghost, like many other doctrines, developed in the centuries following the apostles. The practice is based on Matthew 28:18-19, where we find what is known as the Great Commission:

> ***Matthew 28:18-19*** *And Jesus came and spake unto them, saying, All power is given unto me in heaven and in earth. 19 Go ye therefore, and teach all nations, baptizing them in the name of the Father, and of the Son, and of the Holy Ghost:*

Why, if Jesus commanded baptism in the name of the Father, Son, and Holy Ghost, did his disciples never once baptize this way? The explanation can be found in a careful examination of the Great Commission. Notice that in verse 18 Jesus tells His disciples that all power belongs to Him. Then He starts verse 19 with the word "therefore." The word "therefore" means "because of this fact." Jesus was instructing the disciples to obey the command of verse 19 because He [Jesus] has all power.

Now look carefully at verse 19. Jesus says, "...baptizing them in the name...." The word name here is singular, not plural; Jesus is speaking of only one name, not multiple names. So which name is He referring to? Not "Father," "Son," or "Holy Ghost" because these words are titles, not names. So Jesus is really saying, "Because I have all power, go and baptize in my name." Jesus is the only name that encompasses the titles Father, Son, and Holy Ghost. The disciples of Jesus never baptized using the titles Father, Son, and Holy Ghost because they understood that the name (singular) of the Father, Son, and Holy Ghost is Jesus!

Consider Luke's version of the Great Commission:

> *Luke 24:47 And that repentance and remission of sins should be preached in his name among all nations, beginning at Jerusalem.*

Luke clearly understood that the name of the Father, Son, and Holy Ghost is Jesus, for he said, "...in his name."

It is important to remember that the name of God has had great spiritual significance throughout history. One of the ten commandments forbid the Israelites from taking His name in vain. Hundreds of times throughout the Bible the sacredness of the name is emphasized.

> ***Proverbs 18:10*** *The name of the LORD is a strong tower: the righteous runneth into it, and is safe.*

Was anyone ever rebaptized in the Bible?

Sometimes we are asked if baptism is important enough to require rebaptism in the event that someone was not baptized according to the example set by the apostles. As always, we have to examine what the Bible says on the subject:

> ***Acts 19:1-5*** *And it came to pass, that, while Apollos was at*
> *Corinth, Paul having passed through the upper coasts came to*
> *Ephesus: and finding certain disciples, 2 He said unto them,*
> *Have ye received the Holy Ghost since ye believed? And they*
> *said unto him, We have not so much as heard whether there be*
> *any Holy Ghost. 3 And he said unto them, Unto what then were*
> *ye baptized? And they said, Unto John's baptism. 4 Then said*
> *Paul, John verily baptized with the baptism of repentance,*
> *saying unto the people, that they should believe on him which*
> *should come after him, that is, on Christ Jesus. 5 When they*
> *heard this, they were baptized in the name of the Lord Jesus.*

This passage is significant for several reasons. First, these men were already baptized believers. Second, they weren't baptized by just anybody; they had been baptized by the man who Jesus called the greatest prophet that had ever lived: John the Baptist. Imagine being able to say that you were baptized by John the Baptist himself! Yet Paul recognized that something was missing from their experience, because they had not received the Holy Ghost. The Apostle Paul took baptism in the name of Jesus Christ seriously enough to rebaptize the disciples of John the Baptist!

Chapter 4: The Holy Ghost: What Is It?

I hear a lot of talk about this thing called the Holy Ghost, or Holy Spirit. Just what exactly is it?

First, it is necessary to understand that God, in His essence, is a Spirit. In other words, He does not consist of flesh and bone like you and me. He is not a man, a person, or three persons:

> ***John 4:24*** *God is a Spirit: and they that worship him must worship him in spirit and in truth.*

> ***Numbers 23:19*** *God is not a man, that he should lie...*

Furthermore, there are many evil spirits in the world, but only one that is "holy":

> ***Ephesians 4:4*** *There is one body, and one Spirit, even as ye are called in one hope of your calling;*

Notice that the word "Spirit" in this verse is capitalized, because the Spirit that is referred to is the Holy Spirit. The phrases "Holy Ghost" and "Holy Spirit" are interchangeable and mean exactly the same thing. Both "Ghost" and "Spirit" are identical in the Greek. Both are translated from the Greek word *pneuma*.

Since there is only one Spirit that is holy, this Spirit must be the Spirit of God. When you see phrases in the Bible such as "Spirit of Christ," "Spirit of God," etc. these all refer to the exact same Spirit, the Holy Ghost. There is not a "Spirit of Christ" or "Spirit of God" that is separate from the Holy Ghost, because there is only one spirit (Ephesians 4:4).

The Holy Ghost is nothing mysterious; it is simply God's Spirit at work in us and the world.

Is the Holy Ghost something I can have, and if so, how do I receive it?

The Holy Ghost (God's Spirit living inside of you) is promised to all who believe, repent, and obey the Gospel.

> ***Luke 11:13*** *If ye then, being evil, know how to give good gifts unto your children: how much more shall your heavenly Father give the Holy Spirit to them that ask him?*

> ***Acts 5:32*** *And we are his witnesses of these things; and so is also the Holy Ghost, whom God hath given to them that obey him.*

Be careful to note that the preceding verse promises the Holy Ghost to them that obey Him. The Holy Ghost is not promised to them that "receive" Him or "accept" Him; it is promised to them that obey Him.

> ***Acts 2:38*** *Then Peter said unto them, Repent, and be baptized every one of you in the name of Jesus Christ for the remission of sins, and ye shall receive the gift of the Holy Ghost. 39 For the promise is unto you, and to your children, and to all that are afar off, even as many as the Lord our God shall call.*

The Holy Ghost is not something for which you have to beg, but is something that you simply should expect to receive after you have obeyed God's commands to repent and to be baptized in the name of Jesus Christ.

Doesn't everyone receive the Holy Ghost (Holy Spirit) the moment they believe?

There are several examples of believers who did not have the Holy Ghost. For example, in Acts 8 we read about the Samaritans, a city of believers who had Christ preached to them, received it, heard and saw miracles, had demons cast out of them, were healed, had joy, and were even baptized:

> ***Acts 8:5-17*** *5 Then Philip went down to the city of Samaria,*
> *and preached Christ unto them. 6 And the people with one*
> *accord gave heed unto those things which Philip spake, hearing*
> *and seeing the miracles which he did. 7 For unclean spirits,*

crying with loud voice, came out of many that were possessed with them: and many taken with palsies, and that were lame, were healed. [8] And there was great joy in that city.... [12] But when they believed Philip preaching the things concerning the kingdom of God, and the name of Jesus Christ, they were baptized, both men and women....[14] Now when the apostles which were at Jerusalem heard that Samaria had received the word of God, they sent unto them Peter and John: [15] Who, when they were come down, prayed for them, that they might receive the Holy Ghost: [16] (For as yet he was fallen upon none of them: only they were baptized in the name of the Lord Jesus.) [17] Then laid they their hands on them, and they received the Holy Ghost.

The passage above is clear: the baptized believers in Samaria did not have the Holy Ghost. The Apostles Peter and John went to Samaria to pray for these baptized believers to receive the Holy Ghost.

Notice that these people expected the Holy Ghost to fall. Not only did they not have the Holy Ghost, but they knew they did not have it. Furthermore, those who received the Holy Ghost knew when they had received it. There was a visible sign; even those standing around knew both when others had received it and even when they had not.

These people in Acts 8 had already received the Word of God, believed, repented, received joy, saw miracles, and had even been baptized. Yet none of them had the Holy Ghost, and they all knew it! Clearly, none of the aforementioned items (believing, etc.) in and of itself is proof that one has received the Holy Ghost. However, the Bible does give us clear signs:

Mark 16:17 *And these signs shall follow them that believe; In my name shall they cast out devils; they shall speak with new tongues;*

Tongues were expected to follow the believer.

> ***Acts 2:4*** *And they were all filled with the Holy Ghost, and began to speak with other tongues, as the Spirit gave them utterance.*

> ***Acts 10:45*** *And they of the circumcision which believed were*
> *astonished, as many as came with Peter, because that on the*
> *Gentiles also was poured out the gift of the Holy Ghost. 46 For*
> *they heard them speak with tongues, and magnify God. Then*
> *answered Peter,*

Another example of believers who did not have the Holy Spirit is found in Acts 19, which we looked at earlier when discussing baptism:

> ***Acts 19:1-6*** *And it came to pass, that, while Apollos was at*
> *Corinth, Paul having passed through the upper coasts came to*
> *Ephesus: and finding certain disciples, 2 He said unto them,*
> *Have ye received the Holy Ghost since ye believed? And they*
> *said unto him, We have not so much as heard whether there be*
> *any Holy Ghost. 3 And he said unto them, Unto what then were*
> *ye baptized? And they said, Unto John's baptism. 4 Then said*
> *Paul, John verily baptized with the baptism of repentance,*
> *saying unto the people, that they should believe on him which*
> *should come after him, that is, on Christ Jesus. 5 When they*
> *heard this, they were baptized in the name of the Lord Jesus. 6*
> *And when Paul had laid his hands upon them, the Holy Ghost*
> *came on them; and they spake with tongues, and prophesied.*

This is just one more example of believers who did not have the Holy Ghost.

We mentioned in an earlier lesson that "believing" is the "conception" in the new birth experience. When a person believes, a seed is planted. However, the new birth experience is completed after the unborn child passes through the water (baptism) and receives the Holy Ghost (birth).

Should I try to speak in tongues?

It is unnecessary to "try" to speak in tongues. Furthermore, there is no biblical basis for "teaching" people how to speak in tongues. It is the Spirit that gives the utterance (Acts 2:4).

If you have repented of your sins and been baptized in the name of Jesus Christ like the Samaritans in Acts 8 and the disciples of John the Baptist in Acts 19, you should be open to and expecting the Holy Ghost. Like them, you may be a believer who has never received the Holy Ghost. Since the Holy Ghost is promised to all who obey God, you should expect to receive it and be open to it when it comes. The tongues are simply the result of receiving the Holy Ghost, and the Spirit will cause you to speak. Simply repent of your sins, be baptized in obedience to the Gospel, and believe the promise of God.

While you should not seek to speak in tongues, it is important, however, to seek His Spirit. The Bible is clear that only those who diligently seek Him find Him:

> ***Deuteronomy 4:29*** *...if...thou shalt seek the LORD thy God, thou shalt find him, if thou seek him with all thy heart and with all thy soul.*
>
> ***I Chronicles 28:9*** *...if thou seek him, he will be found of thee;*
>
> ***2 Chronicles 15:12*** *And they entered into a covenant to seek the LORD God of their fathers with all their heart and with all their soul;*
>
> ***Jeremiah 29:13*** *And ye shall seek me, and find me, when ye shall search for me with all your heart.*

While you should not be trying to speak in tongues, it is essential that you seek the Holy Ghost through praise and worship. You pursue Him through praise. Make it a point to worship God with all of your heart every chance you get, and soon you too will find yourself speaking in tongues as the Spirit gives the utterance.

One last point: though you should never attempt to "make" yourself speak in tongues, neither should you resist it. Acts 2:4 says the disciples spoke in tongues "as the Spirit gave them the utterance." The Spirit gave them the words to say, but it was still their tongues, their vocal chords, their lips that did the speaking. The Spirit will move you, but it is up to you to allow the words to come forth using your own lips, tongue, and vocal chords.

What if I do something stupid, silly, or can't stop speaking in tongues?

God will never force you to do anything that you do not want to do. If you want to stop speaking in tongues, you can stop whenever you get ready. However, most find that once they receive the Holy Ghost, they want to continue speaking in tongues as long as they can.

As for acting silly, it is true that many act "drunk," just as Jesus' disciples did on the day of Pentecost, when they receive the Holy Ghost. Many leap for joy from the excitement, some laugh, and some dance. People always tend to get emotional with excitement whenever they receive something special. So it is when you receive the Holy Ghost.

Chapter 5: The Significance of Acts 2:38

Of all the New Testament verses, why is Acts 2:38 so important?

Why is Acts 2:38 so important as a salvation scripture? Why not use Matthew 28:19, John 3:16, Acts 16:31, or the 'Roman Road' to tell someone how to be saved? This chapter deals with this very important issue.

Background to the second chapter of Acts

In order to properly understand the significance of Acts 2:38, one must first have a fundamental understanding of the background preceding the verse. It is imperative that you understand that the Holy Ghost had not yet been given prior to the second chapter of Acts. This is clearly stated in John 7:39:

> *(But this spake he of the Spirit, which they that believe on him should receive: for the Holy Ghost was not yet given; because that Jesus was not yet glorified.)*

While it is true that there were special cases of people who had the Spirit "move upon them" in the Old Testament and even those who were born with the Holy Ghost for special purposes (John the Baptist, for example) in the New Testament, the Holy Ghost had not yet been poured out on all flesh. It was not yet available to all.

Some will argue that Jesus' disciples already had the Holy Ghost prior to Pentecost, and the verse commonly used to support this view is John 20:22:

> *And when he had said this, he breathed on them, and saith unto them, Receive ye the Holy Ghost:*

However, it must be clearly understood that this is a command from Jesus, not a statement – and His disciples fulfilled this command on the day of Pentecost when they actually received the Holy Ghost.

In Luke's version of what happened in John 20:22, we find the following words:

> ***Luke 24:49*** *And, behold, I send the promise of my Father upon you: but tarry ye in the city of Jerusalem, until ye be endued with power from on high.*

If Peter had already received the Holy Ghost prior to Pentecost, he would not have denied Jesus. He would have had the power that Jesus promised in Acts 1:8, and the boldness that enabled him to preach to the crowd on the Day of Pentecost after he received the Holy Ghost. Furthermore, the other disciples would not have forsaken Jesus had they already possessed the power that the Holy Ghost gives.

Note the words of Jesus before He ascended:

> ***Acts 1:8*** *But ye shall receive power, after that the Holy Ghost is come upon you: and ye shall be witnesses unto me both in Jerusalem, and in all Judaea, and in Samaria, and unto the uttermost part of the earth.*

Why would Jesus make such a statement if his disciples already had the Holy Ghost? Furthermore, why even tarry (or wait) at Jerusalem if they already had the Holy Ghost? What were they waiting for?

The Day of Pentecost

> ***Acts 2:1-4*** [1]*And when the day of Pentecost was fully come, they*
> *were all with one accord in one place.* [2] *And suddenly there*
> *came a sound from heaven as of a rushing mighty wind, and it*
> *filled all the house where they were sitting.* [3] *And there*
> *appeared unto them cloven tongues like as of fire, and it sat*
> *upon each of them.* [4] *And they were all filled with the Holy*
> *Ghost, and began to speak with other tongues, as the Spirit*
> *gave them utterance.*

Note that they (the 120 in the upper room) were all filled with the Holy Ghost. The infilling was not selective; every one of the 120 was filled. This is contrary to modern doctrines which teach that the Holy

Ghost is an added blessing given to certain saved people. The Bible never makes this distinction. It automatically assumes that everyone who is born again has the Holy Ghost, and vice versa. The Holy Ghost is not something reserved for a spiritual few; it is for everyone. Acts 5:32 tells us that the Holy Ghost is given to all them who obey Him.

The outpouring in Acts 2 was as the Spirit gave them utterance. This is important because some teach that tongues are "of the devil," but the Bible teaches that true tongues come from the Spirit, so any attempt to attribute tongues to Satanic influences is dangerously close to blasphemy.

As mentioned earlier, it was not "as the Spirit uttered," but "as the Spirit gave them utterance." Some people hinder to free flow of the Holy Ghost through themselves because they are afraid they will say something on their own. However, though it is your vocal chords that speak, it is the Spirit that tells you what to say.

> ***Acts 2:5*** *And there were dwelling at Jerusalem Jews, devout men, out of every nation under heaven)*

Key Point: Those who heard Peter's sermon that day were devout men out of every nation under heaven!

God chose this day (the day of Pentecost) for a specific reason. The feast of Pentecost was a celebration of the completion of the wheat and barley harvests, and people were finally finished harvesting their crops. During Pentecost they brought the first fruits to the temple in Jerusalem for tithes. There was a great multitude of people present here, much more than on most other days, and God chose this day to maximize the effect of the outpouring of the Holy Ghost and Peter's message.

It was important that there was more than just a large crowd present; God planned the outpouring so that devout Jews from all over the world would be present, and these Jews would return to their homes and tell others what they had received in Jerusalem, and what Peter preached.

> ***Acts 2:6-11*** *6 Now when this was noised abroad, the multitude*
> *came together, and were confounded, because that every man*
> *heard them speak in his own language. 7 And they were all*
> *amazed and marvelled, saying one to another, Behold, are not*
> *all these which speak Galilaeans? 8 And how hear we every*
> *man in our own tongue, wherein we were born? 9 Parthians,*
> *and Medes, and Elamites, and the dwellers in Mesopotamia,*
> *and in Judaea, and Cappadocia, in Pontus, and Asia, 10*
> *Phrygia, and Pamphylia, in Egypt, and in the parts of Libya*
> *about Cyrene, and strangers of Rome, Jews and proselytes, 11*
> *Cretes and Arabians, we do hear them speak in our tongues the*
> *wonderful works of God.*

It is sometimes taught that the purpose of the tongues on the day of Pentecost was to preach to the multitudes; however, the problem with this premise is that Greek was the universal language of the day and most likely understood by everyone present, making any other language unnecessary. Furthermore, the scriptures tell us that Peter lifted up his own voice to speak to the people (verse 14), removing any possibility of the tongues being used to preach. Even if the disciples did use tongues to preach to the multitudes (which they did not), such an explanation fails to explain the reason for tongues in Acts 10 or Acts 19, since in each case there was no one to preach to!

> ***Acts 2:12-13*** *12 And they were all amazed, and were in doubt,*
> *saying one to another, What meaneth this? 13 Others mocking*
> *said, These men are full of new wine.*

Some thought the 120 were drunk, further proof that they were not preaching to the multitudes in tongues. If they were simply preaching, no one would have accused them of being drunk.

> ***Acts 2:14-16*** *14 But Peter, standing up with the eleven, lifted up*
> *his voice, and said unto them, Ye men of Judaea, and all ye that*
> *dwell at Jerusalem, be this known unto you, and hearken to my*

words: [15] *For these are not drunken, as ye suppose, seeing it is but the third hour of the day.* [16] *But this is that which was spoken by the prophet Joel;*

Peter identified what they received and did on that day as "that" spoken of by the prophet Joel. Someone once said, "if this is not that, then please tell me what is this and where is that." This statement by Peter is more proof that the Holy Ghost had not yet been poured out on all flesh, since he claimed that the Day of Pentecost, and not earlier, was the fulfillment of Joel's prophecy.

[17] *And it shall come to pass in the last days, saith God, I will pour out of my Spirit upon all flesh:...*

Some teach that the experience that the disciples received on the day of Pentecost is not for everyone. The Bible, however, said God would pour out his Spirit on all flesh.

...and your sons and your daughters shall prophesy, and your young men shall see visions, and your old men shall dream dreams: [18] *And on my servants and on my handmaidens I will pour out in those days of my Spirit; and they shall prophesy:*

Peter begins the conclusion of his sermon later in chapter two with these words:

Acts 2:36-37 [36] *Therefore let all the house of Israel know assuredly, that God hath made that same Jesus, whom ye have crucified, both Lord and Christ.* [37] *Now when they heard this, they were pricked in their heart, and said unto Peter and to the rest of the apostles, Men and brethren, what shall we do?*

KEY POINT: The answer of Peter to these people here is critical. These people would all return to their homelands, their friends, and their families with nothing but what he said at this moment, and what they received today. There was no Matthew 28:19; Matthew had not yet been written. There was no John 3:3 or John 3:5 talking about being born again. These people had never heard of Nicodemus' conversation with Jesus in John 3. There was no John 3:16, no conversion of the Philippian jailor (which would not come until after Paul's conversion, many years later), and no "Roman Road" of salvation; the book of Romans was some thirty years in the future. There was no book of Galatians; it was decades away. **Whatever Peter preached here would become the foundation of the church for the next thirty years, until the books of the Bible began to be written**. It would be the only plan of salvation known to the fledgling Church for that thirty year period!

Peter did not say, "accept Christ as your personal savior," as most churches teach today, so this phrase (or some variation of it) was not going to be the foundational doctrine of the church. Here is Peter's actual response:

> ***Acts 2:38*** *Then Peter said unto them, Repent, and be baptized every one of you in the name of Jesus Christ for the remission of sins, and ye shall receive the gift of the Holy Ghost.*

Some teach that the Holy Ghost is only for a select few, or only those on the day of Pentecost, but notice again the words of Peter:

> 39 *For the promise is unto you, and to your children, and to all that are afar off, even as many as the Lord our God shall call.*

> 42 *And they continued stedfastly in the apostles' doctrine and fellowship, and in breaking of bread, and in prayers.*

What was the *Apostles'* doctrine? Remember: there was no Matthew 28:19, no John 3:16, no epistle to the Romans. Therefore the Apostle's doctrine is Acts 2:38. This is the message that became the foundation of the church, and remains so today.

Chapter 6: Acceptance or Obedience?

Is the phrase, "Accept Christ as your personal Savior" or some variation of it found in the Bible?

One of the most commonly used phrases in the Evangelical Christian world today is "accept Christ as your personal savior" or some variation of this phrase. Unfortunately, the widespread use of this phrase has misled many sincere people into thinking that it is actually found in the Bible. The truth is that these words, and nothing like them, is found in scripture. They have been passed on from person to person down through the years, with very few stopping to carefully study God's Word to find what it really says about salvation. Countless sinners have followed this formula for salvation, only to find themselves still feeling empty on the inside.

What about John 3:16?

> ***John 3:16*** *For God so loved the world, that he gave his only begotten Son, that whosoever believeth in him should not perish, but have everlasting life.*

The major problem with using John 3:16 exclusively as a salvation scripture is that John 3:16, along with the rest of the New Testament, did not exist until some twenty to seventy years after the Day of Pentecost, the birthday of the Church (see the previous chapter on the significance of Acts 2:38). If John 3:16 or any verse other than Peter's message on the Day of Pentecost was the true plan of salvation, then the Church was without a true plan of salvation for at least the first twenty years of its existence!

Another problem with basing salvation solely on John 3:16, without considering the Bible as a whole, is that it is quite possible for a Hindu, Muslim, or Buddhist to believe in Jesus Christ. It is quite possible, for example, for such a person to believe that Jesus Christ was a good man or even a good prophet (most do). This verse, taken by itself, does not require repentance, a belief in the crucifixion, resurrection, or ascension of Jesus Christ. Therefore, John 3:16 is not intended to be a “plan of salvation in a nutshell” verse, but rather is telling us that a person who truly believes in Jesus Christ does not have to perish. John 3:16 does not attempt to explain exactly what “believing in Jesus” actually means.

What does the Bible really say about acceptance?

In fact, the Bible has a lot to say about acceptance. However, what the Bible tells us is what we must do in order to be accepted by God. It tells us nothing about accepting Him. The key is obedience to His Word. When we do what He has told us to do, then we will be accepted by Him, and His acceptance of us is all that matters. Only when He accepts us are we truly saved, and this only occurs through obedience. Let’s examine what the Bible says about acceptance:

> ***Genesis 4:7*** *If thou doest well, shalt thou not be accepted? and if thou doest not well, sin lieth at the door...*

The first occurrence of the word “accepted” is found in the preceding verse. The verse is self-explanatory, in that it is clear that we will be accepted by God if we do well (obey Him).

> ***Genesis 19:21*** *And he said unto him, See, I have accepted thee concerning this thing also, that I will not overthrow this city, for the which thou hast spoken.*

In this verse, God accepts the prayer of Lot. Again, no mention is made of Lot “accepting” God.

> ***Exodus 23:38*** *And it shall be upon Aaron's forehead...that they may be accepted before the LORD.*

God’s laws for Israel were to be followed specifically to ensure that the children of Israel would be accepted by God. No mention is made of them “accepting” Him.

> ***Leviticus 1:4*** *And he shall put his hand upon the head of the burnt offering; and it shall be accepted...*

Burnt offerings made according to God's instructions were guaranteed acceptance by God.

> ***Leviticus 7:18*** *And if any of the flesh of the sacrifice of his peace offerings be eaten at all on the third day, it shall not be accepted...*

> ***Leviticus 19:7*** *And if it be eaten at all on the third day, it is abominable; it shall not be accepted.*

> ***Leviticus 20:20-27*** *[20] But whatsoever hath a blemish, that shall ye not offer: for* ***it shall not be acceptable*** *for you. [21] And whosoever offereth a sacrifice of peace offerings unto the LORD to accomplish his vow, or a freewill offering in beeves or sheep,* ***it shall be perfect to be accepted****...[23] Either a bullock or a lamb that hath any thing superfluous or lacking in his parts, that mayest thou offer for a freewill offering; but for a vow* ***it shall not be accepted****... [25] ...and blemishes be in them:* ***they shall not be accepted for you****... [27] ...and from the eighth day and thenceforth* ***it shall be accepted*** *for an offering made by fire unto the LORD.*

> ***Leviticus 23:11*** *And he shall wave the sheaf before the LORD, to be accepted for you...*

> ***I Samuel 26:19****...If the LORD have stirred thee up against me, let him accept an offering...*

Throughout the Bible, the theme of acceptance by God is overwhelming in its recurrence. Always, it is based upon obedience to His commands.

> ***Deuteronomy 33:11*** *Bless, LORD, his substance, and accept the work of his hands.*

> ***II Samuel 24:23****...And Araunah said unto the king, The LORD thy God accept thee.*

> ***Job 42:9*** *...the LORD also accepted Job.*

Psalms 19:14 *Let the words of my mouth, and the meditation of my heart, be acceptable in thy sight, O LORD...*

Psalms 20:3 *...accept thy burnt sacrifice; Selah.*

Psalm 119:108 *Accept, I beseech thee, the freewill offerings of my mouth, O LORD...*

Proverbs 21:3 *To do justice and judgment is more acceptable to the LORD than sacrifice.*

Ecclesiastes 9:7 *...for God now accepteth thy works.*

Isaiah 56:7 *...their burnt offerings and their sacrifices shall be accepted upon mine altar...*

Isaiah 60:7*...they shall come up with acceptance on mine altar...*

Jeremiah 6:20 *...your burnt offerings are not acceptable...*

Jeremiah 14:10 *...therefore the LORD doth not accept them; he will now remember their iniquity, and visit their sins.*

Jeremiah 14:12 *When they fast, I will not hear their cry; and when they offer burnt offering and an oblation, I will not accept them...*

Ezekiel 20:40-41 *[40] ...there shall all the house of Israel, all of them in the land, serve me: there will I accept them...[41] I will accept you with your sweet savour...*

Ezekiel 43:27 *...the priests shall make your burnt offerings upon the altar, and your peace offerings; and I will accept you, saith the Lord GOD.*

Hosea 8:13 *They sacrifice flesh for the sacrifices of mine offerings, and eat it; but the LORD accepteth them not; now will he remember their iniquity, and visit their sins...*

Amos 5:22 *Though ye offer me burnt offerings and your meat offerings, I will not accept them...*

Malachi 1:10 *...I have no pleasure in you, saith the LORD of hosts, neither will I accept an offering at your hand.*

Malachi 1:13 *...ye brought that which was torn, and the lame, and the sick; thus ye brought an offering: should I accept this of your hand? saith the LORD.*

Some may argue that the dozens of verses relating to acceptance by God are found in the Old Testament, and thus do not apply to us today. Since we are under the dispensation of grace, (or so the argument goes) our obedience has nothing to do with our salvation. Is this true? What does the New Testament have to say on the subject of acceptance? Certainly not that we are to simply “accept Christ,” for this is found nowhere in the New Testament, either. Instead, let’s look at actual verses from the New Testament:

Acts 10:35 *But in every nation he that feareth him, and worketh righteousness, is accepted with him.*

Here Peter declares that fearing the Lord and working righteousness are two requirements for acceptance in His eyes. Simply accepting Him as your personal savior is not enough.

Romans 12:1-2 *[1] I beseech you therefore, brethren, by the mercies of God, that ye present your bodies a living sacrifice, holy, acceptable unto God, which is your reasonable service. [2] And be not conformed to this world: but be ye transformed by the renewing of your mind, that ye may prove what is that good, and acceptable, and perfect, will of God.*

Paul told the Romans that in order for our bodies to be acceptable unto God, they must be a) a living sacrifice, and b) holy.

Romans 14:17-18 *[17] For the kingdom of God is not meat and drink; but righteousness, and peace, and joy in the Holy Ghost.*

[18] For he that in these things serveth Christ is acceptable to God, and approved of men.

Paul is clear that if we serve Christ in righteousness, peace, and joy in the Holy Ghost, we are acceptable to God. Thus we cannot be acceptable to God without the Holy Ghost. This is repeated in the following verse:

***Romans 15:16** ...that the offering up of the Gentiles might be acceptable, being sanctified by the Holy Ghost.*

The offering of the Gentiles (non-Jews) is made acceptable because it is sanctified by the Holy Ghost. How can one possibly be accepted of God without the Holy Ghost, since it is the Holy Ghost that sanctifies our offering?

***II Corinthians 5:9** Wherefore we labour, that, whether present or absent, we may be accepted of him.*

Again, we labor to be accepted by God. Consider what the following verses have to say about being acceptable to God:

***Ephesians 5:10** Proving what is acceptable unto the Lord.*

***Philippians 4:18** But I have all, and abound: I am full, having received of Epaphroditus the things which were sent from you, an odour of a sweet smell, a sacrifice acceptable, wellpleasing to God.*

***I Timothy 2:3** For this is good and acceptable in the sight of God our Saviour;*

***I Timothy 5:4** But if any widow have children or nephews, let them learn first to show piety at home, and to requite their parents: for that is good and acceptable before God.*

***Hebrews 12:28** Wherefore we receiving a kingdom which cannot be moved, let us have grace, whereby we may serve God acceptably with reverence and godly fear:*

> ***I Peter 2:5*** *Ye also, as lively stones, are built up a spiritual house, an holy priesthood, to offer up spiritual sacrifices, acceptable to God by Jesus Christ.*

> ***I Peter 2:20*** *For what glory is it, if, when ye be buffeted for your faults, ye shall take it patiently? but if, when ye do well, and suffer for it, ye take it patiently, this is acceptable with God.*

In each of the seven preceding verses, we are told what is acceptable to God. None mention anything having to do with accepting Christ as savior. In fact, we do not encounter a single verse of scripture even remotely suggesting our "acceptance" of Christ other than II Corinthians 11:4:

> ***II Corinthians 11:4*** *For if he that cometh preacheth another Jesus, whom we have not preached, or if ye receive another spirit, which ye have not received, or another gospel, which ye have not accepted, ye might well bear with him.*

This verse, however, is not talking about accepting *Christ*, but about accepting the *gospel.* In other words, it is not simply the act of accepting Christ into our hearts, as some suggest, but embracing and obeying of the gospel, or good news, of Jesus Christ. This gospel is not only to be believed and accepted, however, but to be obeyed as well.

Ok, I see that I cannot simply accept Christ as my personal savior and be saved. But what else must I do? Exactly what do I have to obey?

You must obey (not just believe) the gospel. The Bible is very clear on this:

> ***Romans 10:16*** *But they have not all* ***obeyed*** *the gospel. For Esaias saith, Lord, who hath believed our report?*

> ***II Thessalonians 1:8*** *In flaming fire taking vengeance on them that know not God, and that* ***obey*** *not the gospel of our Lord Jesus Christ:*

> ***I Peter 4:17*** *For the time is come that judgment must begin at the house of God: and if it first begin at us, what shall the end be of them that* ***obey*** *not the gospel of God?*

I see that I must obey the Gospel, but isn't the Gospel the death, burial, and resurrection of Jesus Christ? How do I obey His death, burial, and resurrection?

It is simple. You must die, be buried, and rise again. When you crucify yourself in repentance, are buried in baptism, and resurrected by the Holy Ghost, you have obeyed the Gospel. Let's look at each of these steps in succession:

First, you must repent. Repentance is confessing past sins, renouncing those sins, and turning to God. It is a change of mind, and a change of attitude. You must purpose in your heart that you will serve God.

But isn't repentance part of believing, or accepting Christ?

For some, it may be. For others, it is not. For example, the drunk or drug addict on skid row may sincerely believe in God, and may believe the gospel. However, he is still bound by sin. He has believed, but he has not obeyed, and there is a distinct difference between the two. Because he has not repented of his sins, he cannot be delivered from them. God demands repentance, and will not set us free through any other means.

Notice that Mark 1:15 tells us to repent and believe:

> ***Mark 1:15*** *And saying, The time is fulfilled, and the kingdom of God is at hand: repent ye, and believe the gospel.*

Repentance is a change of attitude, a change of lifestyle. It encompasses the "obeying" portion of the plan of salvation. Believing, on the other hand, simply means to acknowledge the correctness of something.

It is quite common in many churches to teach that the Holy Ghost comes into a person's heart immediately when that person believes the gospel or "accepts Christ" in to his heart. Does the Bible teach this? Consider Acts 5:32:

> ***Acts 5:32*** *And we are his witnesses of these things; and so is also the Holy Ghost, whom God hath given to them that* ***obey*** *him.*

So Acts 5:32 proves that the Holy Ghost comes not by simple acceptance, but by obedience.

Another example of this principle is found in the eighth chapter of Acts. In this chapter, we find that the people of Samaria heard Christ preached (verse 5), gave heed to preaching (verse 6), heard and saw miracles (verse 6), had joy (verse 8), believed the message (verse 12), and were baptized in the name of the Lord Jesus (verse 16). Yet in spite of all this, they did not have the Holy Ghost (verses 15 and 16). Clearly, none of these things in and of itself is proof of the Holy Ghost.

What else does the New Testament have to say about obedience?

> ***Acts 6:7*** *And the word of God increased; and the number of the disciples multiplied in Jerusalem greatly; and a great company of the priests were* ***obedient*** *to the faith.*

Note that the priests did not merely believe the faith; they were obedient to it.

> ***Romans 1:5*** *By whom we have received grace and apostleship, for* ***obedience*** *to the faith among all nations, for his name:*

> ***Romans 2:5-8*** [5] *But after thy hardness and impenitent heart treasurest up unto thyself wrath against the day of wrath and revelation of the righteous judgment of God;* [6] *Who will render to every man according to his deeds:* [7] *To them who by patient continuance in well doing seek for glory and honour and immortality, eternal life:* [8] *But unto them that are contentious, and do not* ***obey*** *the truth, but obey unrighteousness, indignation and wrath,*

In other words, those who do not obey the truth (verse 8) store up wrath and indignation from God to themselves on the day of wrath and revelation.

> ***Romans 6:17*** *But God be thanked, that ye were the servants of sin, but ye have* ***obeyed*** *from the heart that form of doctrine which was delivered you.*

> ***Galatians 3:1*** *O foolish Galatians, who hath bewitched you, that ye should not* ***obey*** *the truth, before whose eyes Jesus Christ hath been evidently set forth, crucified among you?*

> ***Galatians 5:7*** *Ye did run well; who did hinder you that ye should not* ***obey*** *the truth?*

> ***Philippians 2:12*** *Wherefore, my beloved, as ye have always* ***obeyed****, not as in my presence only, but now much more in my absence, work out your own salvation with fear and trembling.*

> ***Hebrews 5:9*** *And being made perfect, he became the author of eternal salvation unto all them that* ***obey*** *him;*

The writer to the Hebrews declares that Jesus is not the author of eternal salvation to all them that **believe** in Him, but to all them that **obey** Him. See Acts 5:32, which tells us that the Holy Ghost is given to them that obey Him.

> ***I Peter 1:22*** *Seeing ye have purified your souls in* ***obeying*** *the truth through the Spirit unto unfeigned love of the brethren, see that ye love one another with a pure heart fervently:*

Your soul is purified by obeying the truth, not just believing the truth.

Chapter 7: The Necessity of the Holy Ghost

Is the Holy Ghost necessary, or is it just an added blessing for a person who is already saved?

When John the Baptist prophesied of the coming baptism of the Holy Ghost, he did not say it was for some Christians only. He included everyone in his prophecy. Let's take a look at the words of John the Baptist in Matthew 3:11:

> *I indeed baptize you with water unto repentance: but he that cometh after me is mightier than I, whose shoes I am not worthy to bear: he shall baptize you with the Holy Ghost, and with fire:*

It would seem to make sense that if the Holy Ghost was intended for only a select few, but not all saved people, then John would not have made such a blanket statement. He would have said, "he shall baptize some of you with the Holy Ghost...". However, John did not say this. He did not waver or stutter. He included all of his audience in his prophecy.

When Jesus warned his disciples of the persecution to come, He also told them that the Holy Ghost would speak through them. He did not make any exceptions for those who would be "saved" but would not have the Holy Ghost. He assumed that every Christian would have the Holy Ghost.

In Matthew 10:20, Jesus is speaking to his disciples. A pattern begins here that is carried throughout the New Testament: not once does any writer of any book ever speak to two different groups of Christians: those who have the Holy Ghost and those who do not. Every writer of every book assumes every Christian has the Holy Ghost. In the two cases where believers were encountered who did not have the Holy Ghost (Acts 8 and Acts 19), the apostles immediately addressed the deficiency. In neither case was it accepted as a normal condition. **Every** believer was expected to receive the same Holy Ghost that was poured out on the Day of Pentecost.

In Matthew 10:20 and Mark 13:11, Jesus tells his disciples not to worry about what they will say when they are brought before governors and kings, because the Spirit will speak through them:

> ***Matthew 10:20*** *For it is not ye that speak, but the Spirit of your Father which speaketh in you.*

> ***Mark 13:11*** *But when they shall lead you, and deliver you up, take no thought beforehand what ye shall speak, neither do ye premeditate: but whatsoever shall be given you in that hour, that speak ye: for it is not ye that speak, but the Holy Ghost.*

Once again, Jesus treats the subject as automatic; every disciple will have the Holy Spirit. He makes no provision for those who are saved but do not have the Holy Ghost.

Some may argue that there is a difference between the Holy Spirit and the Spirit of Christ or the Spirit of the Father. Does the Bible say so? Look at Ephesians 4:4:

> *There is one body, and one Spirit, even as ye are called in one hope of your calling;*

Since there is only one Spirit, that Spirit must be the Holy Spirit. Matthew 10:20 and Mark 13:11 use the terms "Spirit of your Father" and "Holy Ghost" interchangeably, and the terms "Spirit of Christ" and "Spirit of God" are used interchangeably elsewhere in scripture, proving that they are indeed synonymous:

> ***Romans 8:9*** *But ye are not in the flesh, but in the Spirit, if so be that the Spirit of God dwell in you. Now if any man have not the Spirit of Christ, he is none of his.*

Anywhere in the Bible where the Spirit is mentioned, whether it is the Spirit of Christ, God, or the Father, it is always the Holy Spirit. There is only one Spirit.

The Holy Ghost is given to those who sincerely ask for it, so it is inconceivable that someone could be saved without it.

> ***Luke 11:13*** *If ye then, being evil, know how to give good gifts unto your children: how much more shall your heavenly Father give the Holy Spirit to them that ask him?*

Without the Holy Spirit, you cannot enter the kingdom of God.

> ***John 3:5*** *Jesus answered, Verily, verily, I say unto thee, Except a man be born of water and of the Spirit, he cannot enter into the kingdom of God.*

Some may argue that there is a difference between "receiving" the Holy Spirit, or being "born again," and being "baptized" in or with the Spirit. However, not once does the Bible provide any record of any such distinction. Not once do we read of someone who "receives" the Spirit only to later be "filled" or "baptized" with the Spirit. When the Bible speaks of being "baptized" in or with the Spirit, it means exactly the same thing as being born again.

Jesus prophesied of the coming of the Spirit of Truth, which would dwell in every Christian.

> ***John 14:17*** *Even the Spirit of truth; whom the world cannot receive, because it seeth him not, neither knoweth him: but ye know him; for he dwelleth with you, and shall be in you.*

Keep in mind that every occurrence of Spirit (capital letter S) in the Bible refers to the Holy Spirit, because there is only one Spirit (Ephesians 4:4). Therefore, John 14:17 must refer to the Holy Spirit, and all biblical scholars agree on this. Note that Jesus promised the Holy Spirit to all disciples, not a select few.

The Holy Ghost is our comforter and teacher. It is inconceivable that someone could be a Christian without this teacher, because it teaches us all truth. Without it, you cannot know truth.

> ***John 14:26*** *But the Comforter, which is the Holy Ghost, whom the Father will send in my name, he shall teach you all things, and bring all things to your remembrance, whatsoever I have said unto you.*

> ***John 16:13*** *Howbeit when he, the Spirit of truth, is come, he will guide you into all truth: for he shall not speak of himself; but whatsoever he shall hear, that shall he speak: and he will show you things to come.*

It is not only the Spirit that teaches us truth, but it is the Spirit that empowers us to obey the truth. Without it, you are a slave to sin.

> ***I Peter 1:22*** *Seeing ye have purified your souls in obeying the truth through the Spirit unto unfeigned love of the brethren, see that ye love one another with a pure heart fervently:*

Jesus promised the baptism of the Holy Ghost to all of His disciples, not a select few.

> ***Acts 1:5*** *For John truly baptized with water; but ye shall be baptized with the Holy Ghost not many days hence.*

Jesus identified the Holy Ghost as the source of spiritual power. Without it, you have no power.

> ***Acts 1:8*** *But ye shall receive power, after that the Holy Ghost is come upon you: and ye shall be witnesses unto me both in Jerusalem, and in all Judaea, and in Samaria, and unto the uttermost part of the earth.*

On the day of Pentecost, the Holy Ghost was poured out to all those in the upper room. It was not selective; everyone received it. It is biblical to expect everyone to receive it today.

> ***Acts 2:4*** *And they were all filled with the Holy Ghost, and began to speak with other tongues, as the Spirit gave them utterance.*

The prophet Joel prophesied that the Spirit of the Lord (the Holy Ghost or Holy Spirit) would be poured out on all flesh. It would not be a selective outpouring, but would be available to everyone.

> ***Acts 2:17*** *And it shall come to pass in the last days, saith God, I will pour out of my Spirit upon all flesh: and your sons and your daughters shall prophesy, and your young men shall see visions, and your old men shall dream dreams:*

When Peter preached to the multitudes on the day of Pentecost, he said the Holy Ghost was for anyone who would repent and be baptized in Jesus name. Thus, we can only conclude that those who have not received it have not obeyed his command.

> ***Acts 2:38*** *Then Peter said unto them, Repent, and be baptized every one of you in the name of Jesus Christ for the remission of sins, and ye shall receive the gift of the Holy Ghost.*

This brings us to the main reason that so many believers have never received the Holy Ghost: simply put, they have not fully obeyed God's Word. As simple as it sounds, it is true: many believers have never truly repented, and most believers in the Christian community today have never been baptized in the name of Jesus Christ. True, most have been baptized in the titles Father, Son, and Holy Ghost, but most have not been baptized in the name of Jesus. It is this glaring omission, either through ignorance, neglect, or downright disobedience, that has caused many thousands to miss the joy of the Holy Ghost. If a person truly repents and is baptized in the name of Jesus Christ, he or she is promised the Holy Ghost (Acts 2:38).

The Holy Ghost is promised to all who obey God. If a person does not have the Holy Ghost, he should examine his heart for disobedience.

> ***Acts 5:32*** *And we are his witnesses of these things; and so is also the Holy Ghost,* ***whom God hath given to them that obey him****.*

Perhaps more than any other, this verse proves the necessity of the Holy Ghost. Only those who obey God will receive it. The Holy Ghost and salvation go hand in hand.

When Peter preached to Cornelius' household in Acts 10, everyone who heard the Word received the Holy Ghost. It was not poured out selectively, once again proving it is for everyone.

> ***Acts 10:44*** *While Peter yet spake these words, the Holy Ghost fell on all them which heard the word.*

The love of God is shed abroad in our hearts by the Holy Ghost. It is therefore impossible to have the love of God without the Holy Ghost.

> ***Romans 5:5*** *And hope maketh not ashamed; because the love of God is shed abroad in our hearts by the Holy Ghost which is given unto us.*

When writing to the Romans (and in each of his epistles) Paul assumes that all of his audience has the Holy Ghost. There is no provision in this verse, or any other, for those who are saved but do not have the Holy Ghost, because salvation comes only through the Holy Ghost.

It is the Holy Ghost that takes away the condemnation of sin and makes us free from the law of sin and death. Thus, those who do not have the Holy Ghost are still bound in sin and condemnation.

> ***Romans 8:1-2*** *There is therefore now no condemnation to them which are in Christ Jesus, who walk not after the flesh, but after the Spirit. For the law of the Spirit of life in Christ Jesus hath made me free from the law of sin and death.*

Romans 8:9 clearly tells us that we do not belong to God if we do not have His Spirit.

> ***Romans 8:9*** *But ye are not in the flesh, but in the Spirit, if so be that the Spirit of God dwell in you. Now if any man have not the Spirit of Christ, he is none of his.*

Of course, some will argue that the Spirit of Christ and the Holy Spirit are two different Spirits, but we have already proven from Ephesians 4:4 that there is not but one Spirit, and that the terms "Spirit of

Christ," "Spirit of the Father," "Spirit of God," and "Holy Spirit" are used interchangeably throughout the Bible (compare Matthew 10:20 with Mark 13:11).

The Bible declares that we are complete in Christ:

> ***Colossians 2:8-10*** *[8] Beware lest any man spoil you through philosophy and vain deceit, after the tradition of men, after the rudiments of the world, and not after Christ. [9] For in him dwelleth all the fulness of the Godhead bodily. [10]* ***And ye are complete in him****, which is the head of all principality and power:*

Many churches teach that the Holy Ghost is an added blessing or empowerment that the believer receives after accepting Christ as savior. However, Paul told the Colossians in the preceding verses that they were **complete** in Christ. If the Holy Ghost is something other than the Spirit of Christ, how is it possible to be complete in Christ alone? It isn't possible, of course, proving that the Spirit of Christ and the Holy Spirit are in fact the same Spirit.

All too often it is human nature to make the Bible more complicated than it need be. There are not several different mysterious "Spirits," nor is there a difference in being "filled" with the Spirit and "baptized" with the Spirit. There is one Spirit (God), and either you have Him dwelling within you or you don't.

It is the Holy Spirit that will resurrect us from the dead. Without it, you will not be part of the resurrection of the just.

> ***Romans 8:11*** *But if the Spirit of him that raised up Jesus from the dead dwell in you, he that raised up Christ from the dead shall also quicken your mortal bodies by his Spirit that dwelleth in you.*

Only those who are led by the Spirit are sons of God:

> ***Romans 8:14*** *For as many as are led by the Spirit of God, they are the sons of God.*

The Spirit is our witness that we are children of God:

> ***Romans 8:16*** *The Spirit itself beareth witness with our spirit, that we are the children of God:*

Since the kingdom of God is righteousness, peace, and joy in the Holy Ghost, you cannot be part of the kingdom of God without the Holy Ghost:

> ***Romans 14:17*** *For the kingdom of God is not meat and drink; but righteousness, and peace, and joy in the Holy Ghost.*

Our joy, peace, and hope comes from the Holy Ghost. Without it, we have no joy, peace, or hope:

> ***Romans 15:13*** *Now the God of hope fill you with all joy and peace in believing, that ye may abound in hope, through the power of the Holy Ghost.*

When we submit ourselves to God as a living sacrifice, our offering is sanctified (made pure) by the Holy Ghost. If we do not have the Holy Ghost, we are unacceptable to God:

> ***Romans 15:16*** *That I should be the minister of Jesus Christ to the Gentiles, ministering the gospel of God, that the offering up of the Gentiles might be acceptable, being sanctified by the Holy Ghost.*

It is impossible to know the things of God without the Holy Spirit. Without it, you are wandering in darkness:

> ***I Corinthians 2:11-13*** [11] *For what man knoweth the things of a man, save the spirit of man which is in him? even so the things of God knoweth no man, but the Spirit of God.* [12] *Now we have received, not the spirit of the world, but the spirit which is of God; that we might know the things that are freely given to us of God.* [13] *Which things also we speak, not in the words which man's wisdom teacheth, but which the Holy Ghost teacheth; comparing spiritual things with spiritual.*

Notice once again that Paul assumes everyone in his audience has the Holy Ghost. No provision is made for those who might be saved but do not have the Holy Ghost.

> ***II Corinthians 1:22*** *Who hath also sealed us, and given the earnest of the Spirit in our hearts.*

> ***II Corinthians 4:13*** *We having the same spirit of faith..*

> ***II Corinthians 5:5*** *...God, who also hath given unto us the earnest of the Spirit.*

> ***II Corinthians 11:4*** *For if he that cometh preacheth another Jesus, whom we have not preached, or if ye receive another spirit, which ye have not received...*

> ***Galatians 5:5*** *For we through the Spirit wait for the hope of righteousness by faith.*

> ***II Corinthians 12:18*** *...walked we not in the same spirit? walked we not in the same steps?*

> ***I Thessalonians 1:6*** *And ye became followers of us, and of the Lord, having received the word in much affliction, with joy of the Holy Ghost:*

> ***I Thessalonians 4:8*** *He therefore that despiseth, despiseth not man, but God, who hath also given unto us his holy Spirit.*

> ***II Timothy 1:14*** *That good thing which was committed unto thee keep by the Holy Ghost which dwelleth in us.*

It is the Holy Ghost that makes us the temple (dwelling place) of God. If you do not have the Holy Ghost, you are not the temple of God:

> ***I Corinthians 3:16*** *Know ye not that ye are the temple of God, and that the Spirit of God dwelleth in you?*

> ***I Corinthians 6:19*** *What? know ye not that your body is the temple of the Holy Ghost which is in you, which ye have of God, and ye are not your own?*

We must continue to emphasize that Paul never writes to his audience as though some have the Holy Ghost and some do not. He always assumes everyone has the Spirit of God dwelling within them.

> ***Jude 1:20*** *But ye, beloved, building up yourselves on your most holy faith, praying in the Holy Ghost,*

As Christians, we are washed, sanctified, and justified in the name of the Lord Jesus and by the Spirit, so if we do not have the Spirit we are not washed, sanctified, or justified.

> ***I Corinthians 6:11*** *And such were some of you: but ye are washed, but ye are sanctified, but ye are justified in the name of the Lord Jesus, and by the Spirit of our God.*

No man can truly profess that Jesus is Lord of his life if he does not have the Holy Ghost, so if you do not have the Holy Ghost, Jesus is not Lord of your life.

> ***I Corinthians 12:3*** *Wherefore I give you to understand, that no man speaking by the Spirit of God calleth Jesus accursed: and that no man can say that Jesus is the Lord, but by the Holy Ghost.*

We are baptized into the body of Christ by the Holy Spirit. Thus, someone who does not have the Holy Spirit is not part of the body of Christ.

> ***I Corinthians 12:13*** *For by one Spirit are we all baptized into one body, whether we be Jews or Gentiles, whether we be bond or free; and have been all made to drink into one Spirit.*

The Holy Spirit gives life, so anyone who does not have the Holy Spirit is spiritually dead.

II Corinthians 3:6 *Who also hath made us able ministers of the new testament; not of the letter, but of the spirit: for the letter killeth, but the spirit giveth life.*

Galatians 6:8 *For he that soweth to his flesh shall of the flesh reap corruption; but he that soweth to the Spirit shall of the Spirit reap life everlasting.*

We are "quickened" (made alive) by the Spirit.

I Peter 3:18 *For Christ also hath once suffered for sins, the just for the unjust, that he might bring us to God, being put to death in the flesh, but quickened by the Spirit:*

The Holy Spirit gives us liberty. Without the Holy Spirit, you are still bound in sin.

II Corinthians 3:17 *Now the Lord is that Spirit: and where the Spirit of the Lord is, there is liberty.*

We are changed into the image of God by the Holy Spirit. Without it, you can never hope to attain God's image.

II Corinthians 3:18 *But we all, with open face beholding as in a glass the glory of the Lord, are changed into the same image from glory to glory, even as by the Spirit of the Lord.*

Paul asks the Galatian church rhetorically how they received the Holy Ghost in Galatians 3:2, and answers "by the hearing of faith," confirming that true faith accompanied by repentance will always result in the Holy Ghost:

Galatians 3:2 *This only would I learn of you, Received ye the Spirit by the works of the law, or by the hearing of faith?*

We begin our walk with God in the Spirit (receiving the Holy Ghost). Until you receive the Holy Spirit, you have not truly begun your walk with God.

> ***Galatians 3:3*** *Are ye so foolish? having begun in the Spirit, are ye now made perfect by the flesh?*

It is the Spirit of God that makes us sons of God. Without it, we are not spiritual sons of God.

> ***Galatians 4:6*** *And because ye are sons, God hath sent forth the Spirit of his Son into your hearts, crying, Abba, Father.*

Those who are led by the Spirit are no longer under the Law. Thus it requires the Spirit to free us from the law of sin and death.

> ***Galatians 5:18*** *But if ye be led of the Spirit, ye are not under the law.*

It is the Holy Spirit that seals us, or identifies us as a child of God.

> ***Ephesians 1:13*** *In whom ye also trusted, after that ye heard the word of truth, the gospel of your salvation: in whom also after that ye believed, ye were sealed with that holy Spirit of promise,*

> ***Ephesians 4:30*** *And grieve not the holy Spirit of God, whereby ye are sealed unto the day of redemption.*

It is only through the death of Jesus Christ and by the Holy Spirit that we have access to God.

> ***Ephesians 2:18*** *For through him we both have access by one Spirit unto the Father.*

It is only by the Holy Spirit that we become a habitation (dwelling place) of God. If you do not have the Holy Spirit, God does not dwell within you.

> ***Ephesians 2:22*** *In whom ye also are builded together for an habitation of God through the Spirit.*

Paul understood that his salvation and sanctification (holiness) come through the prayers of the saints and the Holy Spirit.

Philippians 1:19 *For I know that this shall turn to my salvation through your prayer, and the supply of the Spirit of Jesus Christ,*

In other words, Paul's salvation was through the supply of the Spirit. Since there is only one Spirit (Ephesians 4:4), he must be referring to the Holy Spirit.

II Thessalonians 2:13 *...God hath from the beginning chosen you to salvation through sanctification of the Spirit and belief of the truth:*

Salvation comes through sanctification of the Spirit and belief of the truth. It is impossible to be sanctified (made holy) without the Holy Ghost.

Titus 3:5 *Not by works of righteousness which we have done, but according to his mercy he saved us, by the washing of regeneration, and renewing of the Holy Ghost;*

We are saved by the washing of regeneration (baptism - washing) and renewing the Holy Ghost.

Hebrews 10:14-15 *[14] For by one offering he hath perfected for ever them that are sanctified. [15] Whereof the Holy Ghost also is a witness to us: for after that he had said before,*

The Holy Ghost is a witness that we are sanctified (made holy), once again proving that it is impossible to be sanctified without it. This holiness (sanctification) is not our holiness or good works, but His presence in us. It is only through God's Spirit dwelling in us that we can ever be holy in His sight.

I Peter 1:2 *Elect according to the foreknowledge of God the Father, through sanctification of the Spirit, unto obedience and sprinkling of the blood of Jesus Christ: Grace unto you, and peace, be multiplied.*

If the Spirit does not dwell you, God does not dwell in you. It is that simple. There is nothing mysterious about it; either God lives in you or he does not.

> ***I John 3:24*** *And he that keepeth his commandments dwelleth in him, and he in him. And hereby we know that he abideth in us, by the Spirit which he hath given us.*

> ***I John 4:13*** *Hereby know we that we dwell in him, and he in us, because he hath given us of his Spirit.*

Chapter 8: Speaking in Tongues

The first explicit mention of tongues in the Bible is found in Isaiah 28:11:

> ***Isaiah 28:11-12*** *[11] For with stammering lips and another tongue will he speak to this people. [12] To whom he said, This is the rest wherewith ye may cause the weary to rest; and this is the refreshing: yet they would not hear.*

Some have suggested that the Isaiah 28 is prophesying of missionaries that will learn foreign languages. Is this true? No, because Paul used Isaiah's prophecy to teach on the supernatural gift of tongues. He clearly did not believe Isaiah was talking about missionary endeavors.

One of the cardinal rules of biblical interpretation is to allow the Bible to interpret itself when possible. In other words, if a New Testament authority such as Jesus or one of the Apostles quotes a verse from the Old Testament, his interpretation of the Old Testament passage trumps all others. In this particular case, the Apostle Paul actually quotes from this passage twice, so he leaves no doubt as to the meaning of the passage. Paul first quotes from this passage in I Corinthians 14 while teaching a Bible study on the gift of tongues:

> ***1 Corinthians 14:21*** *In the law it is written, With men of other tongues and other lips will I speak unto this people; and yet for all that will they not hear me, saith the Lord.*

The entire 14th chapter of I Corinthians is about speaking in tongues. The fact that Paul quotes it in this chapter tells us that he equates Isaiah 28:11-12 with speaking in tongues. This tells us that Paul understood Isaiah's prophecy to refer to the supernatural use of tongues (the subject of I Corinthians 14).

It is of note that the words *men of* are italicized in I Corinthians 14:21 in the King James text. This means that the words were added by the translators and were not part of the original text. The translation should read:

> *"...With other tongues and other lips will I speak unto this people..."*

This translation is actually closer to what Isaiah actually said, if both verses are compared.

Paul also refers to this passage in Hebrews chapters 3 and 4:

> ***Hebrews 3:11-19*** *[11] So I sware in my wrath, They shall not enter into my rest.) [12] Take heed, brethren, lest there be in any of you an evil heart of unbelief, in departing from the living God...[18] And to whom sware he that they should not enter into his rest, but to them that believed not? [19] So we see that they could not enter in because of unbelief.*

> ***Hebrews 4:1-11*** *Let us therefore fear, lest, a promise being left us of entering into his rest, any of you should seem to come short of it. [2] For unto us was the gospel preached, as well as unto them: but the word preached did not profit them, not being mixed with faith in them that heard it. [3] For we which have believed do enter into rest, as he said, As I have sworn in my wrath, if they shall enter into my rest...[8] For if Jesus had given them rest, then would he not afterward have spoken of another day. [9] There remaineth therefore a rest to the people of God. [10] For he that is entered into his rest, he also hath ceased from his own works, as God did from his. [11] Let us labour therefore to enter into that rest, lest any man fall after the same example of unbelief.*

In this passage Paul teaches us that the "rest" prophesied by Isaiah was in fact the coming of the Holy Ghost. He makes this clear when he states, in Hebrews 4:8:

> *For if Jesus had given them rest, then would he not afterward have spoken of another day.*

What "other day" of rest did Jesus speak of? What was the promise to which Paul referred in Hebrews 4:1? Here it is in Jesus' own words:

> ***Luke 24:49*** [49] *And, behold, I send the promise of my Father upon you: but tarry ye in the city of Jerusalem, until ye be endued with power from on high.*

> ***Acts 1:4-5*** [4] *And, being assembled together with them, commanded them that they should not depart from Jerusalem, but wait for the promise of the Father, which, saith he, ye have heard of me.* [5] *For John truly baptized with water; but ye shall be baptized with the Holy Ghost not many days hence.*

The "other day" of rest to which Paul refers, the "other day" that Jesus spoke of, was the Day of Pentecost, when the promise of the Father was poured out. This was the Holy Ghost that Jesus had promised to His disciples.

Why would God choose to use tongues at all?

First, it is important to understand that God is sovereign. God can do whatever He wishes, and does not need to explain His reasons to us.

That being said, there are at least two biblical reasons that explain why God uses tongues to communicate with man:

1. Since the tongue is the most unruly member of the body, to surrender it to God means you have truly surrendered everything.

   James 3:8 *But the tongue can no man tame; {it is} an unruly evil, full of deadly poison.*

2. The second reason for tongues is that man-made languages may not be adequate to express praise or prayer requests to God:

   Romans 8:26 *Likewise the Spirit also helpeth our infirmities: for we know not what we should pray for as we*

> *ought: but the Spirit itself maketh intercession for us with groanings which cannot be uttered.*

It is no secret that many concepts are not easily expressed in a foreign language. Most languages have words that express a thought or idea better than another language might. When it comes to prayer, native languages often do not suffice, so the Spirit takes over.

Are all supernatural tongues man-made, recognizable languages?

The only place in which the Bible clearly mentions the supernatural use of man-made tongues is Acts 2. The 120 in the upper room spoke in foreign languages unknown to them as the Spirit gave them the utterance. While this passage proves that supernatural tongues *may* be uttered in a earthly language unknown to the speaker, it does not prove that tongues *must* always be recognizable, man-made languages.

The Bible declares, in fact, that there are earthly languages (tongues of men), and heavenly languages (tongues of angels):

> ***I Corinthians 13:1*** *Though I speak with the tongues of men* ***and of angels****, and have not charity, I am become as sounding brass, or a tinkling cymbal.*

Furthermore, the Bible does not tell us that the tongues of Acts 10 and Acts 19 were known languages, and in fact suggests otherwise, since there is no mention of an interpreter or of anyone understanding of the languages.

An example of a heavenly (i.e., not man-made) language is found in Genesis 1:3, where we are told that God said, “Let there be light.” Clearly, man-made languages did not yet exist – so what language did God speak? Throughout the book of Revelation, God and the angels speak to each other and to the saints in heaven. What language did they speak? How will all of the saved out of every nation communicate with each other in heaven? Will a language barrier still exist, or will there be one, universal heavenly language so that saints from China can communicate freely with saints from South America?

Another probable use of a heavenly language to communicate with man is found in Daniel chapter 5. In this chapter king Belshazzar and his lords are having a party when a hand begins to write on the wall. None of the wise (learned) men of the kingdom can interpret the writing, suggesting that the writing was in a language unknown to men at that time. Had it been a common language, such as Chaldee or Hebrew, someone in the kingdom would have been able to read it. However, only the prophet Daniel was ultimately able to interpret the writing through the supernatural power of God's Spirit.

What about scientific research into tongues which proves that tongues are not man-made and therefore not scriptural?

Some have pointed to the existence of so-called "scientific" studies in which individuals were studied while speaking in tongues. The tongues were then compared with all known languages and found not to match any earthly language.

There are several problems with such "studies." To begin with, we have already established that there is no biblical requirement that tongues must be in a known, earthly language, so finding that true tongues are not earthly in nature is not surprising. Furthermore, there are literally thousands of languages and dialects that are now dead (lost and haven't been used for centuries or even millennia), so a person could in fact be speaking one of these languages supernaturally.

It is my opinion that in many cases the tongues spoken in many churches are, indeed, uninspired. Some churches have been known to "teach" people how to speak in tongues and suggest that tongues can be turned on and off at will. However, such abuses do not invalidate the Bible. We should not, as the saying goes, "throw the baby out with the bath water." God will not be intimidated by Satan's attempts to use trickery or sensationalism to discredit Him. He will still speak to His people as He chooses.

Indeed, it is dangerous to be overly critical of tongues even when you suspect that the tongues are not genuine. Jesus identified blasphemy against the Holy Ghost as the only unforgiveable sin (Matthew

12:31), and He did so in response to accusations that His works were inspired by the devil. It is better to leave such cases alone rather than risk misidentifying a genuine moving of the Spirit.

The Day of Pentecost

Acts Chapter 2 describes the first outpouring of the Holy Ghost as promised many times by Jesus and John the Baptist. This outpouring occurred on the Day of Pentecost, and is the event from which "Pentecostal" churches get their name. There were 120 disciples of Jesus present in an upper room in Jerusalem, and all 120 spoke in tongues as they were filled with the Holy Ghost:

> ***Acts 2:1-4*** *And when the day of Pentecost was fully come, they were all with one accord in one place. [2] And suddenly there came a sound from heaven as of a rushing mighty wind, and it filled all the house where they were sitting. [3] And there appeared unto them cloven tongues like as of fire, and it sat upon each of them. [4] And they were all filled with the Holy Ghost, and began to speak with other tongues, as the Spirit gave them utterance.*

The disciples "were sitting" when the outpouring occurred. The Holy Ghost can fall at any time—no altar call necessary. Furthermore, it was as the Spirit gave them utterance. They did not "learn" to speak in tongues, nor did they require practice of any kind. The Spirit empowered them to speak, just as it does today.

Of course, there have been numerous abuses of tongues, just as there have been abuses of just about every other biblical doctrine. However, we cannot discount God's Word just because some have abused it in the past.

The outpouring occurred "when the day of Pentecost was fully come." As we discussed in chapter 5, the feast of Pentecost was a festival attended by as many as 200,000 (some have even suggested a number as high as 1 million) people from around the globe. It was open to "strangers" (Deuteronomy 16:9-13) so there were many present who were not even Jews. The timing was perfect to ensure maximum exposure for the new church. It was important that there was more than just a large crowd present; God planned the outpouring so that devout Jews from all over the world would be present, and these Jews would return to their homes and tell others what they had received in Jerusalem, and what Peter preached.

These new converts (the 3000 souls added to the church) would return home to their native lands **without** a written New Testament at all. They did not have any of the four gospels (Matthew, Mark, Luke, or John). They did not have any of Paul's epistles (Romans, I and II Corinthians, Galatians, etc.). The crowd on the Day of Pentecost did not have any New Testament books for at least 20 years. The Day of Pentecost takes place in approximately 30 AD while the earliest books of the New Testament were written by Paul around 49 or 50 AD.

In other words, Peter's message to the crowds at Pentecost becomes the only New Testament sermon some of these people would hear for this crucial 20 year period. Peter had been given the keys to the kingdom of heaven (Matthew 16:18-19), so he no doubt took this responsibility seriously in unlocking the door to the church.

When the 3000 new converts left Jerusalem, they left with three things:

1. The Old Testament (the common Greek version was called the *Septuagint*), which would have been available in any synagogue and which Jesus preached from. Greek was the universal language of the Roman Empire at the time.

2. The experience they received on the Day of Pentecost; and

3. Peter's sermon.

> [6] *Now when this was noised abroad, the multitude came together, and were confounded, because that every man heard them speak in his own language.*

Even though earthly languages were spoken here, we have already seen that there is no biblical requirement that it must happen this way every time.

> [7] *And they were all amazed and marvelled, saying one to another, Behold, are not all these which speak Galilaeans?* [8] *And how hear we every man in our own tongue, wherein we were born?* [9] *Parthians, and Medes, and Elamites, and the dwellers in Mesopotamia, and in Judaea, and Cappadocia, in Pontus, and Asia,* [10] *Phrygia, and Pamphylia, in Egypt, and in the parts of Libya about Cyrene, and strangers of Rome, Jews and proselytes,* [11] *Cretes and Arabians, we do hear them speak in our tongues the wonderful works of God.*

Were tongues used to preach to the multitudes?

A popular (but erroneous) view is that the 120 only spoke in tongues on the Day of Pentecost in order to preach to the crowds in their native languages. Some have even extended this theory to *every* instance of tongues in the early church, suggesting that tongues are no longer necessary because we now have missionaries who know many foreign languages.

There are several major problems with this view. One problem is that Greek was the *lingua franca* (universal language) of the day and most likely everyone present understood it, making any other language unnecessary. Second, new missionaries have been going into strange lands for centuries, so the need to speak in foreign languages (if that was ever the real reason) has never diminished. Yet the proponents of this view claim that tongues ended with the Apostles.

Another problem is that the Bible tells us that there were 120 (including Mary, the mother of Jesus) who were present and all spoke in tongues. It is not likely that all 120 were preaching at the same time. Furthermore, the scriptures tell us that Peter lifted up his own voice to speak to the people (verse 14). It was he who did the preaching, not the 120. To suggest otherwise is to read something speculative into the text that simply isn't there.

A fourth problem is that the disciples were accused of being drunk (vs. 13). Had they simply been preaching, it is unlikely that they would have been accused of drunkenness. They might have been mocked, laughed at, or dismissed, but it is unlikely that someone would have accused them of drunkenness just for preaching.

Finally, in Acts 10 and Acts 19 tongues are present, yet in each case it is clearly the new converts speaking in tongues, not the preachers. This simple fact alone eliminates any possibility that the primary purpose of tongues was to preach to foreigners.

Continuing with Acts 2, we read:

> 12 *And they were all amazed, and were in doubt, saying one to*
> *another, What meaneth this?*13 *Others mocking said, These men*
> *are full of new wine.* 14 *But Peter, standing up with the eleven,*
> *lifted up his voice, and said unto them, Ye men of Judaea, and all ye that dwell at Jerusalem, be this known unto you, and hearken to my words:*

Since Peter "stood up with the eleven" (vs. 14), and there is no indication of any dispute or disagreement, we must conclude that all twelve disciples approved of his sermon. This is critical, since Peter never mentions "accepting Christ as your personal savior" or simply receiving Him into your heart.

> 15 *For these are not drunken, as ye suppose, seeing it is but the*
> *third hour of the day.* 16 *But this is that which was spoken by*
> *the prophet Joel;*

Peter identified what happened that day (at Pentecost) as "that" spoken of by the prophet Joel:

> 17 *And it shall come to pass in the* ***last days****, saith God,*

Key question: Since Peter identified the Day of Pentecost as the "last days," what time period are we living in, if not the last days?

Some believe that tongues ceased with death of the Apostles, but Joel's prediction was that the outpouring would take place in the *last* days. There are only two possibilities: either we live in the last days, as defined biblically, or the last days are not yet upon us. It is impossible to live "after" the "last" days. Since the prophet Joel predicted the outpouring was to come in the last days, and Peter concurred, identifying the outpouring at Pentecost as the fulfillment of Joel's prophecy, the only remaining possibility is that what happened at Pentecost is for us today.

> *I will pour out of my Spirit upon all flesh:...*

Some believe that the experience that the disciples received on the day of Pentecost is not for everyone. The Bible, however, said God would pour out his Spirit on all flesh. Not all accept it, but it is available to all.

> *...and your sons and your daughters shall prophesy, and your young men shall see visions, and your old men shall dream dreams:* [18] *And on my servants and on my handmaidens I will pour out in those days of my Spirit; and they shall prophesy:*

The conclusion of Peter's sermon:

> ***Acts 2:32-33*** [32] *This Jesus hath God raised up, whereof we all are witnesses.* [33] *Therefore being by the right hand of God exalted, and having received of the Father the promise of the Holy Ghost, he hath shed forth this, which ye now see and hear.*

Jesus told the disciples to go to Jerusalem and wait for the "promise of the Father" (Luke 24:49, Acts 1:4). Peter now identifies what that promise is. Notice that Peter identifies the promise as what they saw and **heard**.

> ***Acts 2:36*** *Therefore let all the house of Israel know assuredly, that God hath made that same Jesus, whom ye have crucified, both Lord and Christ.* [37] *Now when they heard this, they were pricked in their heart, and said unto Peter and to the rest of the apostles, Men and brethren, what shall we do?*

KEY POINT: The answer of Peter to these people here is critical. Recall that these people would all return to their homelands, their friends, and their families with nothing but what he said at this moment, and what they received on that day. There was no Matthew 28:19; Matthew had not yet been written. There was no John 3:3 or John 3:5 talking about being born again. These people had never heard of Nicodemus' conversation with Jesus in John 3. There was no John 3:16, no conversion of the Philippian jailor. The book of Romans was 30 years in the future. There was no book of Galatians; it was decades away. Whatever Peter preached here would be all they knew for the next twenty to thirty years, until the books of the New Testament began to be written and circulated among the churches.

> [38] *Then Peter said unto them, Repent, and be baptized every one of you in the name of Jesus Christ for the remission of sins, and ye shall receive the gift of the Holy Ghost. 39 For the promise is unto you, and to your children, and to all that are afar off, even as many as the Lord our God shall call.*

Peter now offers the same promise, the one he and the other disciples received from Jesus, the Promise of the Father, to his audience.

Cornelius and His Household

In the 10th chapter of Acts the Promise of the Father is poured out on a Gentile (a non-Jew) by the name of Cornelius and his household:

> ***Acts 10:43-44*** [43] *To him give all the prophets witness, that through his name whosoever believeth in him shall receive remission of sins.* [44] *While Peter yet spake these words, the Holy Ghost fell on all them which heard the word.*

Notice that the Holy Ghost ***fell.*** In other words, something visible happened. There were Christian Jews who had made the trip with Peter, and they were under the mistaken impression that the Holy Ghost was only for Jews (not Gentiles). They were amazed to see the Holy Ghost fall on Gentiles:

> [45] *And they of the circumcision* **[the Jews]** *which believed were astonished, as many as came with Peter, because that on the Gentiles also was poured out the gift of the Holy Ghost.*

How did the Jews know that the Gentiles had received it? The next verse tells us:

> [46] *For they heard them speak with tongues, and magnify God.*
> *Then answered Peter,* [47] *Can any man forbid water, that these*
> *should not be baptized, which have received the Holy Ghost as*
> *well as we?* [48] *And he commanded them to be baptized in the*
> *name of the Lord. Then prayed they him to tarry certain days.*

It bears repeating that this is now the third mention of baptism in the Apostolic church, the first two being Acts 2:38 and Acts 8:16. In all three cases baptism is in the name of Jesus.

In Acts 11 Peter is speaking to a group in Jerusalem and relaying what happened to Cornelius and his household:

> ***Acts 11:15-18*** [15] *And as I began to speak, the Holy Ghost fell on them, as on us at the beginning.*

In other words, Peter said, "It happened to Cornelius and his household, just like it happened to us on the Day of Pentecost."

> [16] *Then remembered I the word of the Lord, how that he said,*
> *John indeed baptized with water; but ye shall be baptized with*
> *the Holy Ghost.* [17] *Forasmuch then as God gave them the like*
> *gift as he did unto us, who believed on the Lord Jesus Christ;*
> *what was I, that I could withstand God?* [18] *When they heard*
> *these things, they held their peace, and glorified God, saying,*
> *Then hath God also to the Gentiles granted repentance unto*
> *life.*

The Outpouring of the Holy Ghost on John's Disciples in Acts 19

Acts 19:1-7 *[1] And it came to pass, that, while Apollos was at Corinth, Paul having passed through the upper coasts came to Ephesus: and finding certain disciples,*

These were disciples of John who did not have the Holy Ghost.

[2]He said unto them, Have ye received the Holy Ghost since ye believed? And they said unto him, We have not so much as heard whether there be any Holy Ghost. [3] And he said unto them, Unto what then were ye baptized? And they said, Unto John's baptism. [4] Then said Paul, John verily baptized with the baptism of repentance, saying unto the people, that they should believe on him which should come after him, that is, on Christ Jesus. [5] When they heard this, they were baptized in the name of the Lord Jesus. [6] And when Paul had laid his hands upon them, the Holy Ghost came on them; and they spake with tongues, and prophesied. [7] And all the men were about twelve.

In Acts 2 they were filled; in Acts 10 the Holy Ghost fell; here the Holy Ghost "comes on" the disciples of John.

Because they had not yet been filled, Paul first checked their baptism. Remember the promise of Acts 2:38-39; Paul knew that with repentance (which they had clearly done under John) and baptism in the name of Jesus Christ they were promised the Holy Ghost.

Baptism was significant enough that Paul re-baptized them. This is now the third instance of baptism we've seen where a baptismal formula is mentioned. In all three cases baptism has been in the name of Jesus.

The Samaritan Revival in Acts 8

Acts 8:5-20 *Then Philip went down to the city of Samaria, and preached Christ unto them. [6] And the people with one accord gave heed unto those things which Philip spake, hearing and seeing the miracles which he did. [7] For unclean spirits, crying with loud voice, came out of many that were possessed with them: and many taken with palsies, and that were lame, were*

healed. 8 And there was great joy in that city. 9 But there was a
certain man, called Simon, which beforetime in the same city
used sorcery, and bewitched the people of Samaria, giving out
that himself was some great one: 10 To whom they all gave
heed, from the least to the greatest, saying, This man is the
great power of God. 11 And to him they had regard, because
that of long time he had bewitched them with sorceries. 12 But
when they believed Philip preaching the things concerning the
kingdom of God, and the name of Jesus Christ, they were
baptized, both men and women. 13 Then Simon himself believed
also: and when he was baptized, he continued with Philip, and
wondered, beholding the miracles and signs which were done.
14 Now when the apostles which were at Jerusalem heard that
Samaria had received the word of God, they sent unto them
Peter and John: 15 Who, when they were come down, prayed for
them, that they might receive the Holy Ghost: 16 (For as yet he
was fallen upon none of them: only they were baptized in the
name of the Lord Jesus.) 17 Then laid they their hands on them,
and they received the Holy Ghost. 18 And when Simon saw that
through laying on of the apostles' hands the Holy Ghost was
given, he offered them money, 19 Saying, Give me also this
power, that on whomsoever I lay hands, he may receive the
Holy Ghost. 20 But Peter said unto him, Thy money perish with
thee, because thou hast thought that the gift of God may be
purchased with money.

Here's what we know about the Samaritans in Acts 8:

1. They had Christ preached unto them:

   Then Philip went down to the city of Samaria, and preached Christ unto them. (Verse 5)

Though we aren't told all of the specifics of what Philip preached, we know that it included baptism in the name of Jesus because the Samaritans were baptized in His name.

2. They gave heed (paid attention to) those things which Philip preached, and heard and saw miracles:

   And the people with one accord gave heed unto those things which Philip spake, hearing and seeing the miracles which he did. (Verse 6)

3. Some of them had unclean spirits cast out of them, and many were healed of physical ailments:

   For unclean spirits, crying with loud voice, came out of many that were possessed with them: and many taken with palsies, and that were lame, were healed. (Verse 7)

4. They had great joy:

   And there was great joy in that city. (Verse 8)

5. They were believers, but more than that, they were baptized believers:

   But when they believed Philip preaching the things concerning the kingdom of God, and the name of Jesus Christ, they were baptized, both men and women. (Verse 12)

6. They received the Word of God:

   Now when the apostles which were at Jerusalem heard that Samaria had received the word of God, they sent unto them Peter and John: (Verse 14)

In spite of the fact that the Samaritans were baptized believers who received what was preached to them, had joy, saw unclean spirits cast out, and in many cases were healed, they still did not have the Holy Ghost! By any standard, the Samaritans had "accepted Christ." Yet they *still did not have the Holy Ghost.*

> [15] *Who, when they were come down, prayed for them, that they might receive the Holy Ghost:* [16] *(For as yet he was fallen upon none of them: only they were baptized in the name of the Lord Jesus.) (Acts 8:15-16)*

Several points can be made from verse 16. First, the disciples expected the Holy Ghost to "fall." You can infer exactly what this means from other verses in Acts which speak of the falling of the Holy Ghost, but regardless of how you define the Holy Ghost "falling," it was something visible. The Samaritans knew they did not have the Holy Ghost because they were expecting something visible to take place. It is a fair question to ask what they expected to see, and how the disciples knew they did not have the Holy Ghost. Remember, the Samaritans did not have the Holy Ghost, but equally important, they knew they did not have it. I'll say it one more time: *they were baptized believers who did not have the Holy Ghost!*

However you define the Holy Ghost "falling," it was not simply believing, great joy, healing, accepting Christ, receiving the Word, or being baptized, since the Samaritan had experienced all of this—without the Holy Ghost.

Notice that the Samaritans had been baptized "in the name of the Lord Jesus." This is now the fourth instance of a baptism formula we've seen in this study, and all four were in the name of Jesus. This is especially surprising given that few churches actually baptize this way today.

> [17] *Then laid they their hands on them, and they received the Holy Ghost.*

How did the apostles or the Samaritans themselves know when the Holy Ghost came? Again, there must have been a visible sign.

> [18] *And when Simon saw that through laying on of the apostles' hands the Holy Ghost was given, he offered them money,* [19] *Saying, Give me also this power, that on whomsoever I lay hands, he may receive the Holy Ghost. (Acts 8:17-19)*

It is clear that Simon saw something, for he was willing to pay money for the power to bestow it. Furthermore, Simon was not easily fooled. He was a magician and a master at sleight of hand. He, of all people, would be skeptical of any experience received by the Samaritans; yet he saw something that he could not explain.

Are tongues for the Church today?

Some contend that the supernatural use of tongues ended with the deaths of the Apostles. The scripture usually quoted as a basis for this argument is I Corinthians 13:

> ***1 Corinthians 13:8-12*** *Charity never faileth: but whether there be prophecies, they shall fail; whether there be tongues, they shall cease; whether there be knowledge, it shall vanish away.*
> *[9] For we know in part, and we prophesy in part. [10] But when that which is perfect is come, then that which is in part shall be done away. [11] When I was a child, I spake as a child, I understood as a child, I thought as a child: but when I became a man, I put away childish things. [12] For now we see through a glass, darkly; but then face to face: now I know in part; but then shall I know even as also I am known.*

Clearly, I Corinthians 13 speaks of a day when tongues will cease. But when will that day occur? Or has it already occurred, as proponents of this view claim?

Those who hold the view that tongues have already "ceased" believe that verse 10 is speaking of the Bible when it says "when that which is perfect is come." Their understanding is that the supernatural gifts of the Spirit were only needed until the Bible was completed, around 100 A.D.

In order to understand what I Corinthians 13 is talking about, we have to look at the rest of the passage. Verse 8 also says prophecies will fail [Gr. *katargeo*, "be abolished"]. Are prophecies still valid? Are they still coming true today? If they are, then this passage cannot possibly refer to a time that has already passed. Verse 8 says knowledge will vanish away. Has that happened? Of course not; knowledge is expanding to greater levels than ever before.

In verse 12 Paul says, "For now we see through a glass darkly, but then face to face: now I know in part, but then shall I know even as also I am known." Paul is clearly speaking of heaven, not the Bible, when he says these words. "That which is perfect" refers to heaven, not the Bible.

One rule of biblical interpretation is that every word is to be established in the mouth of two or three witnesses (see Matthew 18:16 and II Corinthians 13:1). Building a doctrine on a single verse is precarious because of the danger of misinterpretation and lack of additional witnesses. If I Corinthians 13:8 is saying that tongues have already ceased, it is the *only* verse in the Bible which says so, giving us one and only one witness.

Paul told the Corinthians that it was his desire that they come behind in no gift while they waited for the coming of the Lord:

> ***1 Corinthians 1:7*** *So that ye come behind in no gift; waiting for the coming of our Lord Jesus Christ:*

In other words, the gifts of the Spirit (including tongues) were to be active in the Church until the coming of the Lord.

Paul told the Ephesians that the five-fold ministry was given until we all come into the unity of the faith:

> ***Ephesians 4:11-13*** *And he gave some, apostles; and some, prophets; and some, evangelists; and some, pastors and teachers; [12] For the perfecting of the saints, for the work of the ministry, for the edifying of the body of Christ: [13] Till we all come in the unity of the faith, and of the knowledge of the Son of God, unto a perfect man, unto the measure of the stature of the fulness of Christ:*

Clearly, the saints are not perfect, the body of Christ still needs edifying, and, with thousands of denominations in Christianity, we are not all in the unity of the faith. Consequently, the offices mentioned in this passage are still needed.

Two of the five offices are those of the apostle and the prophet. Those who believe the Gifts of the Spirit ceased with the deaths of the Apostles also generally believe those two offices died as well (especially since Prophecy is one of the nine spiritual gifts). However, Paul stated that the five offices were given ***until we all come in the unity of the faith***.

Virtually the entire chapters of I Corinthians 12 and 14 are devoted to the proper exercise of the gifts in the church. If the gifts are no longer part of the church, these chapters are essentially wasted space. Yet those who believe tongues have ceased believe the completed Bible eliminates the need for tongues. This would mean that the Bible is teaching us how to use a gift that it (the Bible) eliminated the need for!

Early Church History

While we do not place early church writings on the same par as the Bible, we do believe that they can be helpful in understanding the teachings and doctrines of the day. Numerous early church leaders testify that the gifts of the Spirit were in operation in their own day, decades after the death of the last apostle. Irenaeus (130 AD – 202 AD), the Bishop of Lyons, wrote:

> *"For the prophetical gifts remain with us, even to the present time. And hence you ought to understand that [the gifts] formerly among your nation [the Jews] have been transferred to us."*

This is coming from a man who was born roughly thirty years after the death of the last apostle. Furthermore, because of his status as a bishop, Irenaeus cannot easily be dismissed as a heretic of the time. He speaks with the authority and backing of the church.

The Proper Governance of Tongues in I Corinthians 14

The entire 14th chapter of I Corinthians is dedicated to the proper exercise of tongues in the church. Before we look at this chapter, however, it is important to understand that this chapter is not written to, nor is it written about, sinners who speak in tongues when the Holy Ghost is poured out on them for the first time. The experiences of sinners at conversion are detailed in the book of Acts. The Corinthians were already filled with the Holy Ghost. The 14th chapter of I Corinthians is not intended to address their initial infilling. Instead, it addresses **tongues of praise and worship** as practiced by a Holy Ghost-filled believer, **and the *gift* of tongues**, which is the supernatural ability to receive and deliver a message to the church in tongues.

The chapter begins as follows:

> ***I Corinthians 14:1*** *Follow after charity, and desire spiritual gifts, but rather that ye may prophesy.*

This verse is certainly not prohibiting tongues of worship, the gift of tongues, or any other spiritual gift, but simply establishing that the anointed, preached Word (prophecy) is more important than all other gifts.

On the contrary, the Corinthians are actually encouraged to **desire** spiritual gifts. This is in direct opposition to what many teach.

The Greek word for "prophesy" is *propheteuo*, which means "to speak under inspiration." Unlike tongues, which are always a one-on-one dialogue with God unless an interpreter is involved, prophecy is a message **inspired by God** and directed **to the church**. As we will see later, **tongues of praise and worship** are for your personal benefit. The **gift of tongues, <u>along with an interpreter</u>,** and the **gift of prophecy** benefit the entire body of Christ. Tongues of praise and worship are neither prohibited nor discouraged. Prophecy, however, which benefits the entire body, is the greater gift. Inspired preaching (prophecy) should never take a back seat to tongues unless an interpreter is present (which we will see later).

> [2] *For he that speaketh in an unknown tongue speaketh not unto men, but unto God: for no man understandeth him; howbeit in the spirit he speaketh mysteries.*

This is a clear reference to praising God in tongues. The one speaking in tongues speaks to God. This passage is *not* talking about the *gift* of tongues, which is a message *to the church.*

Once more, to suggest that speaking in tongues is "of the devil" is dangerously close to blasphemy, since the Bible warns us that the speaker speaks to God.

Also, if tongues were solely for the purpose of preaching, and therefore always require an interpreter, as some believe, then the one who speaks in tongues could **never** be said to speak to God. This verse demonstrates that tongues are part of praise and worship, not merely to deliver a message to the church through an interpreter.

This verse also says "no man understandeth him." Earlier we asked whether or not tongues must be an earthly, man-made language. This verse is unequivocal proof that the answer is "no." If tongues were always man-made, it could never be said that no man understands them.

Notice that, unlike some modern critics of tongues, Paul has absolutely no disdain or contempt in his words. There is no haughty use of words like "gibberish" to describe the act of speaking in tongues, as some do in our own day. Paul realizes that communication with God through tongues is a holy and sacred gift and treats the subject with the respect it deserves.

> [3] *But he that prophesieth speaketh unto men to edification, and exhortation, and comfort.*

The one who speaks in tongues speaks to God (vs. 2), but the one who prophesies speaks to men. This is the primary difference between tongues and prophecy, and the reason prophecy is superior unless an interpreter is present. However, neither prophecy nor tongues is forbidden.

> [4] *He that speaketh in an unknown tongue edifieth himself; but he that prophesieth edifieth the church.*

Note that the one who speaks in tongues "edifies," or "encourages" himself or herself in the Spirit. There is absolutely nothing wrong with personal edification. Why would someone *not* want to be edified? Isn't that one of the primary purposes of prayer? Isn't that why people attend church—to draw closer to God in some way? According to verse 4, to deny the use of tongues in church is to deny Christians the freedom of personal edification.

Because prophecy edifies the church and not just one individual, it is superior to tongues of worship; tongues of worship edify an individual, but not the church as a whole. But once again we see that there is nothing in this verse (or any verse, for that matter) that prohibits tongues of worship!

Key Point: Paul says the one who speaks in an unknown tongue edifies himself.

Thus far in I Corinthians 14, we have seen that the one who speaks in tongues speaks to God (vs. 2) and edifies himself (vs. 4). Clearly, tongues are not solely for the purpose of delivering a message to the church. Consequently, **an interpreter is not always necessary**. If you are speaking to God in tongues of praise and worship for the purpose of self-edification , no interpreter is required. Anyone who suggest otherwise is simply not familiar with the subject.

Verse 4 tells us the speaker edifies himself, much like the person who prays privately edifies himself. There is nothing wrong with private prayer which edifies the individual, but public prayer which disrupts the preaching of the Word would be out of order. Likewise, private tongues of praise and worship in the Spirit are never forbidden, but can be disruptive if used unwisely.

> [5] *I would that ye all spake with tongues, but rather that ye prophesied: for greater is he that prophesieth than he that*

speaketh with tongues, except he interpret, that the church may receive edifying.

Here Paul expresses his desire that everyone speak with tongues! This is a far cry from those who discourage or even prohibit speaking in tongues. Think of the vast number of churches today who teach or preach the direct opposite of what Paul states here.

He again reiterates the fact that preaching is superior to tongues, unless the tongues are the gift of tongues followed by interpretation. This is a very important, often overlooked, point: **The gift of tongues, when interpreted, is not inferior to prophecy! Verse 5 declares that a message to the church in tongues, when interpreted, is equal to prophecy in authority, because both edify the church**. In fact, because the very definition of prophecy is "inspired utterance" (a Word from the Lord), tongues + interpretation is a form of prophecy.

So far we have seen the following three uses of tongues:

1. When the Holy Ghost fell on individuals who previously did not have it (Acts 2, Acts 10, Acts 19, and Acts 8).

2. In praise and worship one-on-one with God (I Corinthians 14:2, 4)

3. As a means of delivering a message to the church (I Corinthians 14:5)

6 *Now, brethren, if I come unto you speaking with tongues, what shall I profit you, except I shall speak to you either by revelation, or by knowledge, or by prophesying, or by doctrine?*

Of course, Paul is not suggesting that he did not speak in tongues, since he clearly says later that he spoke in tongues more than anyone else (verse 18). He is simply reemphasizing the point that his personal tongues of praise and worship benefit no one but himself. There is nothing wrong with receiving a private blessing from God, but edifying the church body is better.

> 7 *And even things without life giving sound, whether pipe or*
> *harp, except they give a distinction in the sounds, how shall it*
> *be known what is piped or harped?* 8 *For if the trumpet give an*
> *uncertain sound, who shall prepare himself to the battle?* 9 *So*
> *likewise ye, except ye utter by the tongue words easy to be*
> *understood, how shall it be known what is spoken? for ye shall*
> *speak into the air.*

It appears that the Corinthian church was so focused on tongues that they were neglecting teaching and preaching. When one realizes that tongues are for personal edification, it is easy to see how people could become so "addicted" to tongues that they see no need for preaching or teaching. Perhaps they enjoyed their liberty in the Spirit so much that they felt that they didn't need anything else. Paul, however, emphasizes their need for the Word. Tongues are wonderful, permitted, and even encouraged, but they do not take the place of sound doctrine or the preached Word.

> 10 *There are, it may be, so many kinds of voices in the world,*
> *and none of them is without signification.* 11 *Therefore if I know*
> *not the meaning of the voice, I shall be unto him that speaketh a*
> *barbarian, and he that speaketh shall be a barbarian unto me.*

The word translated "barbarian" here is the Greek word *barbaros*, which simply means "foreigner." It is not intended here as an insult, but simply to identify those who spoke a different language.

Most modern translations say "there are many different languages in the world and none of them is without meaning." In other words, Paul is saying that tongues make sense to someone who understands them or has heard an interpretation, but not to anyone else.

> 12 *Even so ye, forasmuch as ye are zealous of spiritual gifts,*
> *seek that ye may excel to the edifying of the church.*

The Corinthians seemed to have been operating under the same misconception as many today: they were confusing their tongues of praise and worship with the gift of tongues. They thought that simply speaking in tongues meant they had the gift; Paul corrects this notion by letting them know that, unless they are interpreting these tongues, they are for personal edification only. The purpose of the gift of tongues and interpretation is to deliver a message to the church body.

It is obvious that many of the Corinthians were speaking in tongues; otherwise there would have been no need for teaching on the subject. It is equally obvious, for the same reason, that the tongues were seldom interpreted. Since the tongues were seldom interpreted, few of the Corinthians possessed either the gift of tongues or the gift of interpretation. They spoke in tongues in praise and worship, but they did not have the gift that would have empowered them to deliver a message to the church.

> *13 Wherefore let him that speaketh in an unknown tongue pray that he may interpret.*

As stated in the previous note, the Corinthians clearly did not have the gift of tongues and/or interpretation. Paul exhorts them to pray for these gifts.

This verse addresses two common misconceptions:

Some believe that "tongues" in the New Testament refers to foreign languages learned by the speaker to preach to foreign people. In verse 13 above, however, the speaker is already able to speak in tongues. If he can already speak in the foreign language of his audience, why does he need to pray for the gift of interpretation?

The second misconception that Paul addresses here is the notion that tongues in the NT are some miraculous ability to preach to foreigners in their own language, even though the speaker has never learned the language. Again, such a miraculous gift would need no interpretation.

Paul acknowledges that the Corinthians are speaking in tongues, but he does not forbid it. Instead of forbidding them to speak in tongues, he encourages them to pray for the gift of interpretation. It is their misuse of tongues that is the problem, not tongues.

> [14] *For if I pray in an unknown tongue, my spirit prayeth, but my understanding is unfruitful.*

So we see the purpose of praying or worshiping in tongues: the human spirit communicates with God. Once again, nothing in this verse condemns speaking in tongues. Prayer or worship in tongues takes place when the individual is in the spirit.

> [15] *What is it then? I will pray with the spirit, and I will pray with the understanding also: I will sing with the spirit, and I will sing with the understanding also.*

Once again, Paul proves that praying in tongues is normal and appropriate. Since he has already stated that praying in the spirit referred to individual prayer and worship to God (verse 14), here he places his seal of approval on such prayer. Singing in the spirit (in tongues) is also approved, and all of this is different from the gift of tongues and interpretation. Furthermore, Paul does more than simply approve of praying and singing "in the Spirit" (i.e., in tongues); he states that he *himself* will do it.

The only restriction on tongues of praise and worship is that they not interfere with the preaching of the Word and that everything be done decently and in order.

> [16] *Else when thou shalt bless with the spirit, how shall he that*
> *occupieth the room of the unlearned say Amen at thy giving of*
> *thanks, seeing he understandeth not what thou sayest?* [17] *For*
> *thou verily givest thanks well, but the other is not edified.*

Paul says "thou verily givest thanks well," once again sanctioning the practice of speaking in tongues. Tongues of praise and worship are an effective means of edification for the individual, a fact that Paul clearly recognized.

> [18] *I thank my God, I speak with tongues more than ye all:*

Some have suggested Paul meant he spoke in more foreign languages than anyone else, but such a suggestion totally ignores the context of the entire chapter. Such theories are nothing more than desperate attempts to alter Paul's teaching on the subject.

> [19] *Yet in the church I had rather speak five words with my understanding, that by my voice I might teach others also, than ten thousand words in an unknown tongue.*

We have seen nothing yet in this chapter which forbids speaking in tongues of praise and worship to God on an individual basis. We have, in fact, established that such tongues are almost always appropriate. We have also established that such tongues should never supersede the preached Word unless they are interpreted.

In spite of the clear teaching we have already examined, some use the phrase "in the church" in the preceding verse to teach that tongues are not appropriate "in the church" (it is interesting that those who hold this view typically do not believe in or practice speaking in tongues anywhere else, either). However, Paul did not say he would not speak in tongues "in church," nor did he condemn tongues "in church." He simply said he would rather preach than speak in tongues, in church. Furthermore, interpreting verse 19 to preclude the use of tongues in church requires one to ignore the context of the entire chapter. The entire chapter is devoted to the proper exercise of the gift of tongues and interpretation *in the church.* It hardly makes sense to spend verse after verse urging the Corinthians to pray for and seek after the ability to interpret if they will never be allowed to speak in tongues in the presence of others!

> [20] *Brethren, be not children in understanding: howbeit in malice be ye children, but in understanding be men.* [21] *In the law it is written, With men of other tongues and other lips will I speak unto this people; and yet for all that will they not hear me, saith the Lord.*

As part of his lesson on the supernatural gift of tongues, Paul interprets Isaiah 28:11-12, proving that Isaiah is speaking prophetically of tongues, not of missionaries preaching in foreign languages.

> 22 *Wherefore tongues are for a sign, not to them that believe, but to them that believe not: but prophesying serveth not for them that believe not, but for them which believe.*

"Them that believe not" (KJV) in the context of this verse refers not to those who refuse to believe, but rather to those who are not saved, the equivalent of a modern day unsaved visitor.

The Bible in Basic English translates this verse as follows:

> ***1 Corinthians 14:22*** *For this reason tongues are for a sign, not to those who have faith, but to those who have not: but the prophet's word is for those who have faith, and not for the rest who have not.*

Earlier (verse 4) Paul said tongues of individual praise and worship edify the individual. Now he explains how this happens. Tongues of praise and worship are an encouragement to those who are unsaved or weak in faith. Tongues are a powerful confirmation to a sinner seeking the baptism of the Holy Ghost, and a powerful faith-builder to a Christian who is going through a struggle or trial. Specifically because personal tongues edify the individual, they provide encouragement to the one who needs it most, when it is most needed.

Tongues serve the purpose (as they did in Acts 8 to the Samaritans, Acts 10 to the household of Cornelius, and Acts 19 to the disciples of John the Baptist) of providing a visible sign of the Holy Ghost to those who have repented of their sins and obeyed the gospel.

> 23 *If therefore the whole church be come together into one place, and all speak with tongues, and there come in those that are unlearned, or unbelievers, will they not say that ye are mad?*

It is important to take this verse in context with the rest of the chapter. How can we reconcile this verse with verse 22, which says tongues are for a sign "to them that believe not"? The verses seem to contradict one another, with verse 22 promoting tongues as a sign to unbelievers, while verse 23 warns of the negative impact of tongues on unbelievers! This apparent contradiction vanishes once we understand that verse 22 is talking about the tongues that are given to a sinner as a sign of the Holy Ghost, while verse 23 is talking about the tongues of praise and worship of the church body. Likewise, a message in tongues to the church, followed by an interpretation, would not have the same negative effect. However, if the entire church family is speaking in tongues all at once, it may serve as a hindrance to a non-Christian who does not understand.

Thus far, tongues of praise and worship have been approved (see verses 2, 4, 5, 14, 15, and 18), without an interpreter. The key word in this verse (23) is all. Unless prophecy (the anointed, preached Word) goes forth, the service is of no use to the unbeliever.

> [24] *But if all prophesy, and there come in one that believeth not,*
> *or one unlearned, he is convinced of all, he is judged of all:* [25]
> *And thus are the secrets of his heart made manifest; and so*
> *falling down on his face he will worship God, and report that*
> *God is in you of a truth.*

It is interesting that Paul speaks of all prophesying as though it was normal for more than one person to prophesy in a service. Indeed, the entire chapter suggests that the operation of the gifts is something for everyone, not just a select few. The modern church has moved away from the biblical pattern in this respect.

In summary, there are two signs to sinners of the power of God:

1. When the sinner speaks in tongues (verse 22).

2. When the secrets of the sinner's heart are revealed through inspired utterance (preaching, a word of wisdom, a word of knowledge, etc.).

> [26] *How is it then, brethren? when ye come together, every one of you hath a psalm, hath a doctrine, hath a tongue, hath a revelation, hath an interpretation. Let all things be done unto edifying.*

Take turns, and let everything be done in order. There was too much confusion in the Corinthian church, and the danger was that visitors would be put off by the disorganization and harmed by the absence of the prophetic Word.

> [27] *If any man speak in an unknown tongue, let it be by two, or at the most by three, and that by course; and let one interpret.*

One, two, or at most three messages to the church in tongues, with interpretations, are enough in any service. "By course" means "in turn." Those delivering a message to the church in tongues should not interrupt one another, but take turns, if more than one message is given. In my entire lifetime of experience in Pentecostal churches, I've never personally witnessed more than three messages in tongues in a single service.

> [28] *But if there be no interpreter, let him keep silence in the church; and let him speak to himself, and to God.*

To properly understand and interpret the preceding verse, one must have thoroughly studied the first twenty-seven verses in this chapter. By this point, we have clearly established that personal tongues of praise and worship are acceptable and proper. Verse 27 allows for a message to the church in tongues at most three times in a service, and not all at the same time. There should also be an interpreter for a message in tongues to be delivered. In churches where the Holy Spirit moves through tongues and interpretation on a regular basis, there is absolutely nothing mysterious or strange about these verses. When a message in tongues (not the normal tongues of praise and worship) is delivered, everything else in the service shuts down. All music is silenced, all prayer stops, and no one else speaks. The entire sanctuary becomes absolutely silent as everyone waits for the interpretation. Obviously, such a manifestation of the Spirit would be disruptive if repeated over and over again without an interpretation. When verse 28 tells the speaker to keep silence unless an interpreter is present, it also tells him to speak to himself, and to God. This simply means in a low tone of voice, and not in a disruptive manner. "To himself, and to God" is a private conversation, not one that involves the entire church. It is much like two people speaking to one another in a corner of the church after service. **This is not necessarily totally silent**. As we will see later, this same chapter commands women to be silent in church, yet Paul allows for women to sing, prophesy, and pray so clearly "silent" does not mean absolutely silent.

> [29] *Let the prophets speak two or three, and let the other judge.*

In other words, let two or three share their Word from the Lord, while others (probably elders) judge the authenticity of the proclamation.

> [30] *If any thing be revealed to another that sitteth by, let the first*
> *hold his peace.* [31] *For ye may all prophesy one by one, that all*
> *may learn, and all may be comforted.*

As stated earlier, the earliest church services were more participatory, with the gifts more widely used than today. Over the first few centuries of the church Christians increasingly neglected their mandate to exercise the gifts. It has only been in the last century that a revival of the gifts in the church has taken place.

> [32] *And the spirits of the prophets are subject to the prophets.*

With this statement Paul eliminates the "I was in the Spirit and couldn't help myself so I had to take over the church service" excuse. No doubt some were dominating the service and not allowing others to exercise their own gifts.

> [33] *For God is not the author of confusion, but of peace, as in all*
> *churches of the saints.* [34] *Let your women keep silence in the*
> *churches: for it is not permitted unto them to speak; but they*
> *are commanded to be under obedience, as also saith the law.* [35]
> *And if they will learn any thing, let them ask their husbands at*
> *home: for it is a shame for women to speak in the church.* [36]
> *What? came the word of God out from you? or came it unto you*
> *only?*

Women were allowed to sing, pray, and prophesy (see I Corinthians 11:5), so virtually no one is suggesting that Paul means absolute silence since this would prevent women from teaching Sunday School, singing in the choir, etc. He is addressing order in the church, not issuing a blanket decree of total silence. The same principle applies to tongues in verse 28, where Paul also tells the speaker to be silent.

> 37 *If any man think himself to be a prophet, or spiritual, let him acknowledge that the things that I write unto you are the commandments of the Lord.* 38 *But if any man be ignorant, let him be ignorant.* 39 *Wherefore, brethren, covet to prophesy, and forbid not to speak with tongues.*

This is one of the clearest commands in scripture: forbid not to speak with tongues. Any teacher or preacher who forbids others to speak with tongues or teaches against tongues is in direct violation of God's Word.

> 40 *Let all things be done decently and in order.*

This is a summary of the entire chapter. As long as tongues are used properly and as designed by God, for a message from God (the gift of tongues and interpretation), or through non-disruptive praise and worship, they are in order.

Chapter 9: The Godhead

What is the single most important doctrine in the Bible?

What if you were asked this question: What is the single most important thing a Christian must believe? Suppose you asked a dozen strangers in a typical Christian church on a Sunday morning the same question. What do you think they would say? What would your answer be? Many would respond with answers such as the resurrection, the virgin birth of Jesus, or that Jesus was the Son of God. In fact, Jesus Himself **was** asked that very question, and answered it for us.

Before we hear how Jesus answered this question, we need to examine a little history, back to the time of Moses. The world of 3200 years ago was very different from today. The Egyptians had gods almost without number — sufficient for every day in the year. There was the powerful god Osiris and the beautiful goddess Isis. There were deities represented by the ibis (a wading bird native to Egypt), dogs, cats, cattle, and hawks. The Hittites, another race of people, had a thousand gods, including the sun god, the sky god, and the storm god. In China, during the Shang dynasty, ancestors were worshiped. The early Pueblo Indians in North America worshiped the Father and Earth Mother, war gods, sky serpents, the spider woman, and many more.

But something earth-shaking happened 3200 years ago. In the midst of this world of thousands of gods, a man named Moses went up on a mountain in the desert of the Sinai peninsula. He did not eat or drink for 40 days, and when he descended from the mountain, he had in his hands a set of laws. Perhaps the most startling of those laws was what the Jews, to this day, refer to as the central declaration of their faith, the Shema:

Shema Yisrael Adonai Eloheynu Adonai Echad

Which is rendered in English as:

> ***Deuteronomy 6:4*** *Hear, O Israel: the Lord our God {is} one Lord:*

Such a proclamation sent shockwaves through the world of that time. The idea of a single, all-powerful God was a unique concept. Never before had an entire nation of people accepted, or even contemplated, the possibility that there was absolutely one, and only one, all powerful God. In one fell swoop one of the great religions of the world was born.

Of course, the God of Moses had always existed. Individual men like Noah, Abraham, Isaac, and Jacob had worshiped him long before Moses was born. But these men were unique; they were the exception rather than the rule. There was no "one-god" religion in the world. The idea of monotheism as a religion was utterly novel.

Now we jump ahead twelve hundred years into the future, where another man is approached by a Jewish scribe and asked a simple question: What is the single greatest commandment God ever gave? The man who was questioned by the scribe, and who answered the question for us, was none other than Jesus himself:

> ***Mar 12:28-34*** [28] *And one of the scribes came, and having heard them reasoning together, and perceiving that he had answered them well, asked him, Which is the first commandment of all?* [29] *And Jesus answered him,* ***The first of all the commandments is, Hear, O Israel; The Lord our God is one Lord****:* [30] *And thou shalt love the Lord thy God with all thy heart, and with all thy soul, and with all thy mind, and with all thy strength: this is the first commandment.* [31] *And the second is like, namely this, Thou shalt love thy neighbour as thyself.* ***There is none other commandment greater than these****.* [32] *And the scribe said unto him, Well, Master, thou hast said the truth: for* ***there is one God; and there is none other but he…***[34] *And when Jesus saw that he answered discreetly, he said unto him, Thou art not far from the kingdom of God..*

It is important to note that Jesus did not simply say that believing in the absolute oneness of God is important; **He said it is the most important commandment of all**. In other words, when it comes to believing, Jesus was declaring that it is essential to get that understanding right before moving on to anything else.

Furthermore, when the scribe reiterated the oneness of God in his response to Jesus' answer, Jesus did not "correct" Him or attempt to explain a mysterious trinity to the man. Instead, He praised the man for his understanding, and told him that, based on his response, he was not far from the kingdom of God.

For thousands of years after Moses, Jews like this scribe accepted, without question, the simple fact that God was absolutely one. Yet today, many in Christianity struggle with this concept. The most common description of God is "three in one," or "one God in three persons." Many, however, find this description to be counterintuitive, with most calling it a "mystery." This chapter examines this important subject.

I have heard some people say God is a trinity of three persons. Is God a person, a group of persons, or a spirit?

In the statement of faith of many churches you will find something along the lines of "God is a Trinity eternally existent in three persons." Such language is a holdover from thousand-year-old creeds, but has no basis in the Bible. Instead, the Bible declares that God is a *spirit*. He revealed Himself to us in the person of Christ Jesus, but He is most definitely not a group of "persons." As a matter of fact, the word "trinity" is not found in the Bible. Instead, the Bible tells us exactly what God is in John 4:24:

> ***John 4:24*** *God {is} a Spirit: and they that worship him must worship {him} in spirit and in truth.*

So God is not a group of persons. He is a Spirit who revealed Himself to us in the person of Jesus Christ. Jesus Christ was fully God manifested (or revealed) in the flesh:

> ***1Timothy 3:16*** *[16] And without controversy great is the mystery of godliness:* ***God was manifest in the flesh****, justified in the Spirit, seen of angels, preached unto the Gentiles, believed on in the world, received up into glory.*

Some people speak of the Holy Spirit, and the Spirit of God, and the Spirit of Christ. Just how many Spirits are there?

There is only one Spirit of God. There are not two Spirits, or three Spirits. See Ephesians 4:4:

> ***Ephesians 4:4*** *{There is} one body, and one Spirit, even as ye are called in one hope of your calling;*

Notice that "Spirit" is spelled with a capital "S," which denotes the Holy Spirit. Of course there are many evil spirits, spelled with a lowercase “s,” and there are human spirits as well. However, there is only one Spirit (capital “S”) of God. There is only one spirit that is Holy.

Since there is only one Spirit, God and the Holy Spirit and the Spirit of Christ are all one and the same. Furthermore, since God is a spirit, He does not consist of flesh and bones, as Jesus said in Luke:

> ***Luke 24:39*** *Behold my hands and my feet, that it is I myself: handle me, and see; for a spirit hath not flesh and bones, as ye see me have.*

Has anyone ever seen God?

Not as a spirit, in the fullness of His glory. He told Moses:

> ***Exodus 33:20*** *And he said, Thou canst not see my face: for* ***there shall no man see me, and live****.*

God’s glory is simply too great for man to witness. The fact that no one has seen God in His glory, or in His essence, is repeated many times in the Bible:

John 1:18 *No man hath seen God at any time…*

John 5:37 *And the Father himself, which hath sent me, hath borne witness of me. Ye have neither heard his voice at any time,* ***nor seen his shape****.*

Colossians 1:15 *Who is the image of the* ***invisible*** *God, the firstborn of every creature:*

1 Timothy 1:17 *Now unto the King eternal, immortal,* ***invisible****, the only wise God, {be} honour and glory for ever and ever. Amen.*

1 Timothy 6:16 *Who only hath immortality,* ***dwelling in the light which no man can approach unto; whom no man hath seen, nor can see****: to whom {be} honour and power everlasting. Amen.*

1 John 4:12 *No man hath seen God at any time.*

If no man has seen God at any time, then who was Jesus?

Clearly, many people saw Jesus during His earthly ministry. The Bible is also clear that Jesus is God. So how can it be possible that no one has seen God, if Jesus was (and is) God?

Whenever the Bible speaks of the Father, it is referring to God in His Spirit form. Jesus (the man) was God the Father dwelling in a fleshly body. In other words, He was God revealing Himself to us in a way we could comprehend. Jesus is the image (picture) of an invisible God, as Colossians 1:15 says:

Colossians 1:15 Who is the image of the invisible God*, the firstborn of every creature:*

The **man** Christ Jesus was God in a human body. Hundreds of years before the birth of Jesus, Isaiah prophesied that the Father would come to earth as a child:

> ***Isaiah 9:6*** *For unto us a child is born, unto us a son is given: and the government shall be upon his shoulder: and his name shall be called Wonderful, Counsellor, the Mighty God, the Everlasting* ***Father****, the Prince of Peace.*

The Apostle John spoke of the Word which was in the beginning and became flesh for us:

> ***John 1:1*** *In the beginning was the Word, and the Word was with God, and the Word was God.*

> ***John 1:3*** *All things were made by him; and without him was not any thing made that was made.*

> ***John 1:14*** *And the Word was made flesh, and dwelt among us, (and we beheld his glory, the glory as of the only begotten of the Father,) full of grace and truth.*

> ***Colossians 1:16*** *For by him [Jesus] were all things created, that are in heaven, and that are in earth, visible and invisible, whether {they be} thrones, or dominions, or principalities, or powers: all things were created by him, and for him:*

> ***John 10:30*** *I and {my} Father are one.*

In the 14th chapter of John, Philip, one of Jesus' disciples, asked Him to show the Father to them:

> ***John 14:8-9*** *Philip saith unto him,* ***Lord, shew us the Father, and it sufficeth us. [9] Jesus saith unto him, have I been so long time with you, and yet hast thou not known me, Philip****? he that hath seen me hath seen the Father; and how sayest thou {then}, Shew us the Father?*

In other words, Jesus' reply to this request from Philip was to tell Philip that He (the Father, in the person of Jesus Christ) was already with them and had been for a long time. There was no one else to show. Everything the Father was or ever had been was fully revealed in Jesus Christ.

Consider the words of Paul in his letter to the Colossians:

> ***Colossians 2:9*** *For in him* [Christ] *dwelleth* ***all*** *the fulness of the Godhead bodily.*

Most churches teach that Jesus is part of a three-part Godhead. They teach that Jesus is God the Son, and that He is just one of the three members of the Trinity (the other two being God the Father and God the Holy Ghost). They teach that all three together comprise the Godhead.

But notice that Colossians 2:9 does not say that Jesus dwells in the Godhead (like most churches teach); it says **all** of the Godhead (Father, Son, and Holy Ghost) dwells **in Jesus**. This is a major distinction. Jesus is not "part" of some mysterious Trinity. He is God fully revealed to mankind. He is the personification of the Father, Son, and Holy Ghost.

> ***1 Timothy 3:16*** *And without controversy great is the mystery of godliness: God was manifest in the flesh, justified in the Spirit, seen of angels, preached unto the Gentiles, believed on in the world, received up into glory.*

Notice that Paul, in the preceding words to Timothy, did not say that the Son was manifested in the flesh (as most churches teach), but instead said that God Himself was manifested in the flesh. Jesus was not part of God; He was everything that is God.

> ***John 8:58*** *Jesus said unto them, Verily, verily, I say unto you, Before Abraham was, I am.*

The phrase "I AM" would have been readily recognizable to any Jew in Jesus' day. It was God's divine name revealed to Moses in Exodus 3:14. In fact, the Jews understood the significance of Jesus' claim so clearly that they picked up stones to stone Him for blasphemy! They clearly understood that He was claiming to be the God of Abraham, Isaac, Jacob, and Moses.

> ***Matthew 1:23*** *Behold, a virgin shall be with child, and shall bring forth a son, and they shall call his name Emmanuel, which being interpreted is, God with us.*

> ***Acts 20:28*** *Take heed therefore unto yourselves, and to all the flock, over the which the Holy Ghost hath made you overseers, to feed the church of God, which he hath purchased with his own blood.*

It is clear from all of the preceding verses that God prepared a body for Himself in order to live among men. Paul mentions this body in Ephesians 4:4:

> ***Ephesians 4:4 {There is} one body****, and one Spirit, even as ye are called in one hope of your calling;*

That body was the Son that was begotten (born).

> ***John 3:16*** *For God so loved the world, that he gave his only* ***begotten*** *Son, that whosoever believeth in him should not perish, but have everlasting life.*

The Son (the man Christ Jesus) walked the earth for thirty-three years. During this time, it was the Father/God/Spirit that gave the Son/man/flesh life and power. While the traditional view of the Trinity is that the Father, Son, and Holy Ghost are coequal and coeternal, the Scriptures teach that the Son was born (John 3:16) and had less power than the Father:

> ***Joh 5:26*** *[26] For as the Father hath life in himself;* ***so hath he given to the Son to have life in himself;***

> ***John 5:19*** *Then answered Jesus and said unto them, Verily, verily, I say unto you,* ***the Son can do nothing of himself****, but what he seeth the Father do: for what things soever he doeth, these also doeth the Son likewise.*

> ***John 6:57*** *As the living Father hath sent me, and* ***I live by the Father****: so he that eateth me, even he shall live by me.*

> ***John 14:28*** *Ye have heard how I said unto you, I go away, and come {again} unto you. If ye loved me, ye would rejoice, because I said, I go unto the Father:* ***for my Father is greater than I.***

God the Father, who cannot die, did not die on the cross; rather, His body, the Son, died on the cross. Furthermore, if the Father volunteered a second member of a Trinity to go to the cross, that would not be love, but cowardice. However, to manifest, or wrap, Himself in flesh and die for our sins represents the highest form of love. In fact, I Timothy 3:16 teaches us that He (God) did just that:

> ***1 Timothy 3:16*** *And without controversy great is the mystery of godliness:* ***God was manifest in the flesh****, justified in the Spirit, seen of angels, preached unto the Gentiles, believed on in the world, received up into glory.*

So it is evident that Jesus is the Father according to the Spirit and the Son according the flesh. Father and Son are inseparably one according to Isaiah:

> ***Isaiah 9:6*** *For unto us a child is born, unto us a* ***son*** *is given: and the government shall be upon his shoulder: and his name shall be called Wonderful, Counseller, The mighty God,* ***the everlasting Father****, The Prince of Peace.*

> ***John 14:8-9*** *Philip saith unto him, Lord, shew us the Father, and it sufficeth us. 9 Jesus saith unto him, have I been so long time with you, and yet hast thou not known me, Philip? he that hath seen me hath seen the Father; and how sayest thou {then}, Shew us the Father?*

> ***John 10:30*** *I and {my} Father are one.*

Where does the Holy Ghost fit into all of this?

Many people are surprised to discover that the Father of the baby Jesus was actually the Holy Ghost!

> ***Matthew 1:18*** *Now the birth of Jesus Christ was on this wise: When as his mother Mary was espoused to Joseph, before they came together,* ***she was found with child of the Holy Ghost****.*

> ***Matthew 1:20*** *But while he thought on these things, behold, the angel of the Lord appeared unto him in a dream, saying, Joseph, thou son of David, fear not to take unto thee Mary thy wife: for* ***that which is conceived in her is of the Holy Ghost****.*

> ***Luke 1:35*** *And the angel answered and said unto her,* ***the Holy Ghost shall come upon thee****, and the power of the Highest shall overshadow thee: therefore also that holy thing which shall be born of thee shall be called the Son of God.*

Therefore, if Jesus is the Father revealed in flesh, then the Spirit of Christ must also be the Holy Spirit, since the Holy Ghost and the Father are the same spirit! This is proven in John 14:16-18, 26:

> ***John 14:16*** *And I will pray the Father, and he shall give you another Comforter, that he may abide with you for ever;*

> ***John 14:17*** *{Even} the Spirit of truth; whom the world cannot receive, because it seeth him not, neither knoweth him: but ye know him;* ***for he dwelleth with you, and shall be in you****.*

> ***John 14:18*** *I will not leave you comfortless:* ***I will come to you****.*

Since there can only be one Spirit (Ephesians 4:4), the Spirit of Christ and the Holy Spirit are identical. In fact, the terms "Spirit of God," "Spirit of Christ," "Spirit of the Father," and "Holy Spirit" are used interchangeably throughout the Bible.

> ***Romans 8:9*** *But ye are not in the flesh, but in the Spirit, if so be that the Spirit of God dwell in you. Now if any man have not the Spirit of Christ, he is none of his.*

To summarize, Jesus was both God and man, divine and human. He possessed a human will that He had to subject to will of the Father (remember His prayer in Gethsemane "not my will, but thine be done"). Jesus ate, slept, rested, and felt pain, all as a man. But He was also God manifested in the flesh.

Furthermore, each of us is created in the image of God (Genesis 1:27). Each of us consists of spirit and flesh, just as God Himself did in the man Christ Jesus. However, we are not each three separate persons, and neither is God.

Isaiah declared that there is only one Savior:

> ***Isaiah 43:10-11*** *Ye {are} my witnesses, saith the Lord, and my servant whom I have chosen: that ye may know and believe me, and understand that I {am} he: before me there was no God formed, neither shall there be after me. [11] I, {even} I, {am} the Lord; and beside me {there is} no saviour.*

However, Luke 2:11 clearly calls Jesus the Savior, so Jesus must be the Father of the Old Testament, the only Savior!

> ***Luke 2:11*** *For unto you is born this day in the city of David a Saviour, which is Christ the Lord.*

Some common questions:

Question: Who is God talking to in Genesis 1:26 when He says, "Let us make man in our image, after our likeness..."?

Answer: Several key points are in order:

1. Jesus is called the Logos (Word) that became flesh in John 1. In John's day the Logos was understood to be the divine thoughts, plan, will, or reason of God. The **man** Christ Jesus always existed as the divine plan (Logos) of God, since God is not bound or limited by space and time. Whatever exists in the plan of God is reality and is as good as done, though it may be centuries in the future from a human time scale.

2. The Old Testament prophets often spoke of the Messiah in the past tense. For example, David declared of Jesus that "they

pierced my hands and my feet" (Psalm 22:16). Isaiah said, "He was wounded for our transgressions" (Isaiah 53:5) centuries before Jesus was born. There are too many examples to mention, but suffice it to say that Old Testament prophets declared New Testament events as though they had already happened because in God's master plan they were as good as done.

3. The Bible speaks of the Lamb slain "from the foundation of the world" even though Jesus was not literally crucified until around 30 A.D. Once again, this is because He was crucified ("slain") in the Logos (plan) of God from the beginning. In the mind and plan of God, it was as good as done, so the Bible can speak of it as though it was completed even before time as understood by humans began.

4. The New Testament speaks of the Son as the "firstborn of every creature" (Colossians 1:15). The word "firstborn" comes from the Greek word *prototokos*, from which we get "prototype."

In Genesis 1, the Son existed as the Logos (word, plan, purpose) of God. The Son was the prototype of what God wanted every man to be. He did not yet exist *in the flesh* since He had not yet been born, but was already predestined in the mind and plan of God, just as it could be said that He was "slain from the foundation of the world" centuries before He was actually crucified. We have already seen that God is a Spirit (John 4:24) so God, being invisible, did not actually have an "image" to make man according to. Furthermore, we saw that Colossians 1:15 declares Jesus to be the "image of the invisible God," yet this image did not exist until Jesus was born. So when God says "let *us* make man in our image, after our likeness" He is speaking of making man *according to the image that was to be born in Bethlehem thousands of years in the future.*

Question: Who was Jesus praying to in the Garden of Gethsemane?

Answer: This passage of scripture is a powerful refutation of the doctrine of the Trinity, since the doctrine of the Trinity asserts that the three persons in the Godhead are co-equal as well as co-eternal. If such is case, why is the Son praying to the Father? Remember, Jesus himself said that His Father was greater than He:

> ***John 14:28*** *Ye have heard how I said unto you, I go away, and come {again} unto you. If ye loved me, ye would rejoice, because I said, I go unto the Father: for my Father is greater than I.*

Again, we have to understand that Jesus was both divine and human. As God, he was divine, and hence raised the dead, opened blind eyes, etc. As man, however, he grew tired, felt pain, and hungered. As the Son He was human, while as the Father He was God almighty. In the Garden of Gethsemane the Son (humanity) prayed to the Father (deity) because it was the Son who would suffer and needed strength, not the Father. It was the Son who had a will that had to be subjected to the will of the Father, so that Jesus prayed, "not my will, but thine be done" (Luke 22:42). This was certainly not the prayer of a co-equal, co-eternal, Second Person in the Godhead. This was not the prayer of a " junior God" who was perfectly one in unity with the Father. It was the prayer of a man, a man with feelings, a man with a will that had to be suppressed. The Son died on the cross. The Father, on the other hand, could not die, because He is God as a Spirit. This also explains Jesus' otherwise inexplicable dying words on the cross, "My God, My God, why hast thou forsaken me?" Jesus, the man, in his greatest moment of suffering and exhaustion, felt the Spirit (the Father) leave his body so that he could die. It was the Father that gave the Son life (John 5:26), so as long as the Spirit inhabited the Son, which was the outward image of the invisible God, the body could not die.

Question: Why does Matthew 28:19 tell us to be baptized in the name of the Father, Son, and Holy Ghost?

Answer: Matthew 28:19 is what is commonly referred to as "The Great Commission." It is Jesus' command to evangelize the world, and the command was given to His disciples just before He ascended into heaven. All four gospel witnesses (Matthew, Mark, Luke, and John) recorded the Great Commission. Let's look at how each of them remembered the words of Jesus.

Matthew 28:18-19 reads:

> ***Matthew 28:18-19*** [18] *And Jesus came and spake unto them, saying, All power is given unto me in heaven and in earth.* [19] *Go ye therefore, and teach all nations, baptizing them in the name of the Father, and of the Son, and of the Holy Ghost:*

Matthew's version of the Great Commission begins in verse 18 with Jesus telling His disciples that **all** power has been given to Him. He then proceeds to tell them to "Go ye therefore…" The word "therefore" means "because of this." In other words, Jesus says, "I have all power, so go teach." It hardly makes sense that Jesus would say, "I have power, so go teach in the names of two others persons."

Second, notice that the word "name" in this passage is singular, denoting one name. It is not talking about two or three names. Third, Father, Son, and Holy Ghost are all three titles, not names. So Jesus is clearly talking about **one** name, a name that fits all three titles (Father, Son, and Holy Ghost). As we have seen from multiple passages, the name of Jesus Christ is the only name that fits.

Mark's version of the Great Commission commands baptism, but doesn't mention a baptismal formula:

> ***Mark 16:16*** *He that believeth and is baptized shall be saved; but he that believeth not shall be damned.*

Luke's version states the following, in Luke 24:47:

> ***Luke 24:47*** *And that repentance and remission of sins should be preached in his name among all nations, beginning at Jerusalem.*

Pay close attention to how Luke heard and interpreted the Great Commission: the preaching was to be in *his name*—Jesus! Luke could not be any clearer about what name Jesus was talking about in Matthew 28:19.

According to Acts 2:38, remission of sins is accomplished through baptism:

> ***Acts 2:38*** *Then Peter said unto them, Repent, and be baptized every one of you in the name of Jesus Christ for the remission of sins, and ye shall receive the gift of the Holy Ghost.*

Therefore, Luke 24:47 is clearly referring to baptism in Jesus' Name.

Finally, John's take on the Great Commission is particularly interesting. John 20:23 mentions the remission of sins again:

> ***John 20:23*** *Whose soever sins ye remit, they are remitted unto them; {and} whose soever {sins} ye retain, they are retained.*

In the Great Commission, John understood Jesus to be giving His disciples the authority to remit (forgive) sins. Obviously, Jesus' disciples could not forgive sins, but they could remit sins by baptizing converts.

It is significant that not one person in the Bible was ever baptized in the titles Father, Son, and Holy Ghost! Everyone in the Book of Acts (the only book of the Bible which is a historical record of the early church) was baptized either in the name of the Lord, the name of the Lord Jesus, the name of Jesus, or the name of Jesus Christ. Any truly honest person will have to admit that the disciples of Jesus obviously understood Matthew 28:19 to mean the name of Jesus, the only name which signifies the Father, Son, and Holy Ghost.

Question. Acts 7:55-56 states that Stephen saw Jesus standing on the right hand of God. What does this mean?

Answer: When the Bible speaks of the "right hand" of God, it is always figurative, since we have already proven that God is a spirit and as such does not have a literal arm or hand. For example, when the Bible speaks of the heart of God, it is referring to His intellect and His emotions, not an organ made of tissue:

> ***Genesis 6:6*** *And it repented the LORD that he had made man on the earth, and it grieved him at his heart.*

> ***Genesis 8:21*** *And the LORD smelled a sweet savour; and the LORD said in his heart...*

If we interpret every physical description of God in the Bible as being literal, then we must believe that God has feathers and wings, and that He has horns coming out of His hands:

> ***Psalms 91:4*** *He shall cover thee with his feathers, and under his wings shalt thou trust: his truth shall be thy shield and buckler.*

> ***Habakkuk 3:4*** *And his brightness was as the light; he had horns coming out of his hand: and there was the hiding of his power.*

Other figurative verses speak of smoke coming out of His nostrils. Of course, God does not have literal nostrils.

> ***2 Samuel 22:9*** *There went up a smoke out of his nostrils, and fire out of his mouth devoured: coals were kindled by it.*

The "right hand" is a figure of speech used to emphasize power, as is often done even today. For example, when we speak of a strong supporter, he is called a "right-hand man".

> ***Exodus 15:6*** *Thy right hand, O LORD, is become glorious in power: thy right hand, O LORD, hath dashed in pieces the enemy.*

> ***Psalms 17:7*** *Show thy marvellous lovingkindness, O thou that savest by thy right hand them which put their trust in thee from those that rise up against them.*

> ***Psalms 20:6*** *Now know I that the LORD saveth his anointed; he will hear him from his holy heaven with the saving strength of his right hand.*

> ***Psalms 98:1*** *A Psalm. O sing unto the LORD a new song; for he hath done marvellous things: his right hand, and his holy arm, hath gotten him the victory.*

The right hand of God is even spoken of as having a mind and will of its own:

> ***Psalms 21:8*** *Thine hand shall find out all thine enemies: thy right hand shall find out those that hate thee.*

> ***Psalms 45:4*** *...thy right hand shall teach thee terrible things.*

Moses blessed Israel with a song about the Law coming as a bolt of fire from God's right hand (another figurative passage):

> ***Deuteronomy 33:2*** *And he said, The LORD came from Sinai, and rose up from Seir unto them; he shined forth from mount Paran, and he came with ten thousands of saints: from his right hand went a fiery law for them.*

Isaiah said that God's right hand spans the universe (if these verses are to be taken literally, and not figuratively), so Stephen would have had to be able to see billions of miles to see Jesus standing at the right hand of God!

> ***Isaiah 48:13*** *Mine hand also hath laid the foundation of the earth, and my right hand hath spanned the heavens: when I call unto them, they stand up together.*

Now let's review some key points. We have already established conclusively from multiple verses that no man has ever seen, nor can see, God (John 1:18 and I John 4:12). No man can see God's glory and live (Exodus 33:20). Second, God is a Spirit (John 4:24) and a Spirit does not have flesh and bones (Luke 24:39) and hence can't be seen. If all of this is true, how could Acts 7:55 say Stephen saw the glory of God and Jesus standing on the right hand of God? Simple; Acts 7:55-56 was never intended to be taken literally. It is figurative, like the many passages that speak of God's heart, nostrils, breath, etc. Stephen saw a vision of God. What did the vision represent, since it could not possibly be literal without directly contradicting scripture? Matthew 26:64 and Mark 14:62 both speak of the "Son of Man" sitting on the right hand of power:

> ***Matthew 26:64*** *Jesus saith unto him, Thou hast said: nevertheless I say unto you, Hereafter shall ye see the Son of man sitting on the right hand of power, and coming in the clouds of heaven.*

> ***Mark 14:62*** *And Jesus said, I am: and ye shall see the Son of man sitting on the right hand of power, and coming in the clouds of heaven.*

Throughout His earthly ministry, Jesus spoke of being subordinate to the Father. As the Son, He depended on the Father for His very life (John 5:26).

However, Jesus also frequently prophesied of His own "glorification." For example:

> ***Luk 24:26*** *[26] Ought not Christ to have suffered these things, and to enter into his glory?*

> ***Joh 7:39*** *[39] (But this spake he of the Spirit, which they that believe on him should receive: for the Holy Ghost was not yet given; because that Jesus was not yet glorified.)*

> ***Joh 12:14-16*** *[14] And Jesus, when he had found a young ass, sat thereon; as it is written, [15] Fear not, daughter of Sion: behold, thy King cometh, sitting on an ass's colt. [16] These things understood not his disciples at the first: but when Jesus was glorified, then remembered they that these things were written of him, and that they had done these things unto him.*

> ***Joh 12:23*** *[23] And Jesus answered them, saying, The hour is come, that the Son of man should be glorified.*

What does the Bible mean when it speaks of the "glorification" of Jesus? Once Jesus completed His earthly calling and conquered death, hell, and the grave at Calvary, He arose in power. The distinction between Father (deity) and Son (humanity) was erased, because Jesus was now "glorified." He could truly say, in Matthew 28:18, that "**all** power is given unto me." After His glorification there was nothing about the Father or Holy Ghost that was not in Jesus Christ. Paul spoke of it this way:

> ***Colossians 2:9-10*** *[9] For in him dwelleth all the fulness of the Godhead bodily. [10] And ye are complete in him, which is the head of all principality and power:*

In other words, **all** of the Godhead (Father, Son, and Holy Ghost) is now embodied in Jesus Christ. Paul even went on to say "ye are **complete** in Him, which is the head of **all** principality and power" (vs. 10). If the Father is separate from Jesus, Paul could not say "ye are complete" in Christ. Paul could not make such a statement if the Holy Ghost is a separate person in the Godhead. Nor could Paul declare Jesus the head of **all** principality and power, if in fact He is sharing that power with the Father and the Holy Ghost.

Since the phrase "right hand" has always represented power, and the term "Son of man" throughout the Bible represents the humanity of Jesus, Stephen saw a vision in which Christ Jesus took His rightful place on the throne of God. Anywhere in the Bible where it appears to refer to a Father and Son as two separate persons, it always includes a word or phrase to clarify that the Son of which it speaks is the man Christ Jesus. Note that Acts 7:56 states that Stephen saw the Son of man standing on the right hand of God (not the right hand of the Father). The phrases "right hand of the Father" and "Father's right hand" do not appear in the Bible, because the phrase "right hand" is indicative of **all** of the power of God, not just that belonging to one third of a mysterious Trinity. Thus we can only conclude that this passage symbolizes the status inherited by the Son when he ascended into heaven; that is, he inherited all of the power accompanying the Spirit. He no longer had to say, "my Father is greater than I." He no longer had to say, "I live by the Father" or "the Son can do nothing of Himself." He was now glorified, and possessed all power previously constrained to the Father. Jesus spoke of this momentous event in Matthew 28:18, and gives us the reason we are to baptize in His (Jesus') name, which encompasses the Father, Son, and Holy Ghost:

> ***Matthew 28:18*** *18 And Jesus came and spake unto them, saying, All power is given unto me in heaven and in earth.*

Jesus was speaking these words after His glorification. Now He could truly say He had all power, without limitation.

Question. Why is it important to believe in the Oneness of God?

Answer. We take on the name of Jesus when we are baptized in His name. No one in the Bible was ever baptized in the titles Father, Son, and Holy Ghost; everyone was baptized either in the name of Jesus, Jesus Christ, or the Lord Jesus (Acts 2:38, 8:16, 19:5). The name of Jesus is the only name under heaven given among men whereby we must be saved:

> ***Acts 4:12*** *Neither is there salvation in any other: for there is none other name under heaven given among men, whereby we must be saved.*

> ***Acts 10:43*** *To him give all the prophets witness, that* ***through his name*** *whosoever believeth in him shall receive remission of sins.*

The name of Jesus in baptism brings remission of sins (Acts 2:38 and 10:43). Furthermore, we are the Bride of Christ if we are in the Church, and a bride always takes on the name of her husband.

Problems with Traditional Trinitarian Doctrine

So far in this chapter we have devoted ourselves to a defense of the oneness of God as expressed in Jesus Christ. In so doing, we have answered many major questions that are commonly asked. However, can the traditional Trinitarian concept of God be defended biblically? The following section will present a series of thought-provoking questions which will help to settle the issue.

The Trinitarian viewpoint is that there is one God in three distinct and separate persons: God the Father, God the Son, and God the Holy Ghost. According to classical Trinitarianism, these three are one in unity (agreement), co-equal in power, and co-eternal (all three have always existed). Jesus, as God the Son, is but one of the three, and is separate and distinct from God the Father and God the Holy Ghost. All three have a will that is in perfect agreement one with another.

Adherents to the doctrine of the absolute oneness of God, on the other hand, teach that there is one God, and that He fully revealed Himself to us in the singular person of Jesus Christ. We believe that Jesus had a dual nature, that is, He was both God (the Father) and man (the Son). Since Jesus was both divine (Spirit) and human (flesh) and we are created in His (God's) image, we are also dual in nature – we have a body and a spirit. Granted, our nature is fallen because of sin, but in the original plan of God Jesus was the prototype of the man God intended all of us to be. Through the shed blood of Jesus Christ we can take on His nature.

The following questions illustrate the problems with the Trinitarian viewpoint:

1. If Jesus is not the Father, explain Isaiah 9:6:

   Isaiah 9:6 *For unto us a child is born, unto us a son is given: and the government shall be upon his shoulder: and his name shall be called Wonderful, Counseller, The mighty God, the everlasting Father, The Prince of Peace.*

2. If Jesus is not the Father, explain John 14:8:

   John 14:8-9 *Philip saith unto him, Lord, shew us the Father, and it sufficeth us. [9] Jesus saith unto him, have I been so long time with you, and yet hast thou not known me, Philip? he that* *hath seen me hath seen the Father; and how sayest thou {then}, Shew us the Father?*

3. Are Father, Son, and Holy Ghost names or titles? If they are titles, then what is the name of the Father, Son, and Holy Ghost?

Matthew 28:19 *Go ye therefore, and teach all nations, baptizing them in the name of the Father, and of the Son, and of the Holy Ghost:*

4. How many names are referenced in Matthew 28:19, above? Remember, the word "name" is singular, not plural.

5. If Jesus is not the Father, Son, and Holy Ghost, then why did all of His disciples interpret Matthew 28:19 (where the term "name", not "names" is used) to mean the name of Jesus Christ when they baptized?

Acts 2:38 *Then Peter said unto them, Repent, and be baptized every one of you in the name of Jesus Christ for the remission of sins, and ye shall receive the gift of the Holy Ghost.*

Acts 8:16 *(For as yet he was fallen upon none of them: only they were baptized in the name of the Lord Jesus.)*

Acts 10:48 *And he commanded them to be baptized in the name of the Lord. Then prayed they him to tarry certain days.*

Acts 19:5 *When they heard {this}, they were baptized in the name of the Lord Jesus.*

6. Why is not one person in the entire Bible ever baptized in the name of the Father, Son, and Holy Ghost, if this is the correct formula in baptism?

7. Some suggest that it is *acceptable* to baptize converts in the name of Jesus Christ since He is, in their view, one-third of the divine Trinity. According to this line of thinking, it is equally acceptable to baptize in the name of the Father, in the name of the Holy

Ghost, or in the name of all three, since any of the above represents the Trinity. If this is true, one would expect that about one-third of the baptisms in Acts would have been administered in the name of the Father, about one-third in the name of Jesus, and about one-third in the name of the Holy Ghost. However, **all** were administered in the name of Jesus Christ. Why?

8. If the baptismal formula is not important, as some teach, then is it important that we immerse people in water rather than sprinkling them? If so, why is it important? Isn't it because that is the way is was done in the Bible? Why, then, do we not baptize in the name of Jesus Christ, since that is the way it was done in the Bible?

9. We know that Matthew, Mark, Luke, and John are four versions of Jesus' life and ministry. Why does Luke, in his version of Matthew 28:19, interpret the name of the Father, Son, and Holy Ghost to be Jesus?

Luke 24:47 *And that repentance and remission of sins should be preached in his name among all nations, beginning at Jerusalem.*

10. The following passage states that there is no savior besides Jehovah (the Father). How is this possible unless Jesus, the savior, is also Jehovah, the Father?

Hosea 13:4 *Yet I {am} the Lord thy God from the land of Egypt, and thou shalt know no god but me: for {there is} no saviour beside me.*

Isaiah 43:10-11 *Ye {are} my witnesses, saith the Lord,and my servant whom I have chosen: that ye may know and believe me, and understand that I {am} he: before me there was no God formed, neither shall there be after me.* [11] *I, {even} I, {am} the Lord; and beside me {there is} no saviour.*

11. The Bible teaches us that the baby Jesus was conceived of the Holy Ghost (Matt. 1:20). If this is true, then the Holy Ghost is the true father of Jesus. Yet Jesus refers to the Father as "my Father"

many times (Matt. 7:21, 10:32-33, 11:27, 12:50, and 16:17 to name a few). If the Father and the Holy Ghost are not the same Spirit, then who is the real father of Jesus?

12. The Oneness view is that the Father was greater than the Son, since the Father was deity and the Son was God revealed in humanity. The Trinitarian view is that the Father and Son are both persons in a triune Godhead who have always been equal in power. If they are equal in power, explain the following verses:

    John 14:28 *Ye have heard how I said unto you, I go away, and come {again} unto you. If ye loved me, ye would rejoice, because I said, I go unto the Father:* ***for my Father is greater than I.***

    John 5:19 *Then answered Jesus and said unto them, Verily, verily, I say unto you,* ***The Son can do nothing of himself, but what he seeth the Father do****: for what things soever he doeth, these also doeth the Son likewise.*

    John 5:26 *For as the Father hath life in himself; so hath he given to the Son to have life in himself;*

    John 8:28 *Then said Jesus unto them, When ye have lifted up the Son of man, then shall ye know that I am {he}, and {that}* ***I do nothing of myself****; but as my Father hath taught me, I speak these things.*

    Mark 13:32 *But of that day and {that} hour knoweth no man, no, not the angels which are in heaven,* ***neither the Son****, but the Father.*

13. If the Father and Son were equal, who was Jesus praying to in the Garden of Gethsemane?

14. If the Son was the Second Person in the Godhead, who died on the cross? Did God die? Or was it a man (the human manifestation of the one God)?

15. If the Father, Son, and Holy Ghost are all three spirits, then there is more than one Spirit. Explain Ephesians 4:4:

    Ephesians 4:4 *{There is} one body, and one Spirit, even as ye are called in one hope of your calling;*

16. What did Jesus' dying words on the cross (in Matt. 27:46) mean?

    Matthew 27:46 *And about the ninth hour Jesus cried with a loud voice, saying, Eli, Eli, lama sabachthani? that is to say, My God, my God, why hast thou forsaken me?*

17. If the Son is eternal (the Trinitarian viewpoint) how could he be born (begotten)?

    John 3:16 *For God so loved the world, that he gave his only* ***begotten*** *Son, that whosoever believeth in him should not perish, but have everlasting life.*

18. If God the Father is a loving Father, why would he offer His son to die, rather than Himself?

    1 Timothy 3:16 *And without controversy great is the mystery of godliness: God was manifest in the flesh, justified in the Spirit, seen of angels, preached unto the Gentiles, believed on in the world, received up into glory.*

19. If Jesus does not fully contain **all** that is God, explain the following verse:

    Colossians 2:8-9 *Beware lest any man spoil you through philosophy and vain deceit, after the tradition of men, after the rudiments of the world, and not after Christ.* [9] *For in him dwelleth all the fulness of the Godhead bodily.*

20. If there are three persons in heaven in the Godhead, why did John the Revelator see only one throne?

Revelation 4:2 *And immediately I was in the spirit: and, behold, a throne was set in heaven, and {one} sat on the throne.*

21. If "God the Son" is our mediator with God the Father, then why does the following verse use the phrase, "the man Christ Jesus?"

1 Timothy 2:5 *For {there is} one God, and one mediator between God and men, the* ***man*** *Christ Jesus;*

Romans 5:15 *But not as the offence, so also {is} the free gift. For if through the offence of one many be dead, much more the grace of God, and the gift by grace, {which is} by one* ***man****, Jesus Christ, hath abounded unto many.*

22. If the baptismal formula is not important enough to warrant rebaptism, why did Paul instruct John's disciples to be re-baptized?

Acts 19:3-5 *And he said unto them, Unto what then were ye baptized? And they said, Unto John's baptism.* [4] *Then said Paul, John verily baptized with the baptism of repentance, saying unto the people, that they should believe on him which should come after him, that is, on Christ Jesus.* [5] *When they heard {this}, they were baptized in the name of the Lord Jesus.*

23. If Jesus is God the Son, and is equal to God the Holy Ghost, then why is it unforgivable to blaspheme the Holy Ghost but not the Son?

Matthew 12:32 *And whosoever speaketh a word against the Son of man, it shall be forgiven him: but whosoever speaketh against the Holy Ghost, it shall not be forgiven him, neither in this world, neither in the {world} to come.*

24. If Jesus was God the Son before his birth, and already had all power as God, why is all power given to the Son in Matthew 28:18, and who gave it to Him? If it was the Father, then He had to have more power than the Son in the beginning.

Matthew 28:18 *And Jesus came and spake unto them, saying, All power is given unto me in heaven and in earth.*

25. Who is the Comforter promised in John 14? Is it the Holy Ghost, as taught by Trinitarian doctrine? If so, then why does Jesus say it is Himself in verse 18?

John 14:16-18 *And I will pray the Father, and he shall give you another Comforter, that he may abide with you for ever;* [17] *{Even} the Spirit of truth; whom the world cannot receive, because it seeth him not, neither knoweth him:* ***but ye know him; for he dwelleth with you, and shall be in you.*** [18] ***I will not leave you comfortless: I will come to you.***

26. In Revelation 22, who sends His angel to His servants, the Lord God of the holy prophets or Jesus? Is this because Jesus <u>is</u> the Lord God of the holy prophets?

Revelation 22:6 *And he said unto me, These sayings {are} faithful and true: and the Lord God of the holy prophets sent his angel to shew unto his servants the things which must shortly be done.*

Revelation 22:16 *I Jesus have sent mine angel to testify unto you these things in the churches. I am the root and the offspring of David, {and} the bright and morning star.*

27. Since we are created in the image of God, why do we not consist of three persons each?

Genesis 1:27 *So God created man in his {own} image, in the image of God created he him; male and female created he them.*

28. Since the Trinitarian viewpoint is that God the Father, God the Son, and God the Holy Ghost are completely and totally one in unity, and thus can logically have only one will, why did Jesus pray in the Garden of Gethsemane, "not my will, but thine be done" to the Father? If, as the Son, he had no will outside that of the Father, then this prayer would have been meaningless. If

however, the will of the flesh differed from the will of the Spirit, this verse can be easily explained.

Additional verses for study:

Isaiah 44:6 *Thus saith the Lord the King of Israel, and his redeemer the Lord of hosts; I {am} the first, and I {am} the last; and* ***beside me {there is} no God****.*

Isaiah 44:8 *Fear ye not, neither be afraid: have not I told thee from that time, and have declared {it}? ye {are} even my witnesses.* ***Is there a God beside me? yea, {there is} no God; I know not {any}.***

Isaiah 45:5-6 I {am} the Lord, and {there is} none else, {there is} no God beside me… {there is} none beside me. I {am} the Lord, and {there is} none else.

Isaiah 45:21 *...* ***{there is} no God else beside me; a just God and a Saviour; {there is} none beside me.***

Hosea 13:4 *Yet I {am} the Lord thy God from the land of Egypt, and thou shalt know no god but me****: for {there is} no saviour beside me.***

Psalms 71:22 *... O thou Holy* ***one*** *of Israel.*

Psalms 78:41 *Yea, they turned back and tempted God, and limited the Holy* ***One*** *of Israel.*

Hosea 11:9 *... or I {am} God, and not man; the Holy* ***One*** *in the midst of thee...*

Habakkuk 3:3 *God came from Teman, and the Holy* ***One*** *from mount Paran. Selah. His glory covered the heavens, and the earth was full of his praise.*

Malachi 2:10 *Have we not all one father? hath not* ***one*** *God created us...*

Mark 12:32 *... there is* ***one*** *God; and* ***there is none other but he:***

Romans 3:30 *Seeing {it is}* ***one*** *God, which shall justify the circumcision by faith...*

1 Corinthians 8:4 *...* ***{there is} none other God but one.***

Galatians 3:20 *...God is* ***one****.*

James 2:19 *Thou believest that there is* ***one*** *God; thou doest well: the devils also believe, and tremble.*

Deuteronomy 6:4 *Hear, O Israel: the Lord our God {is} one Lord:*

Psalms 89:18 *...the Holy* ***One*** *of Israel is {our} king.*

Isaiah 1:24 *Therefore saith the Lord, the Lord of hosts, the mighty* ***One*** *of Israel, Ah, I will ease me of mine adversaries, and avenge me of mine enemies:*

Isaiah 5:24 *...they have cast away the law of the Lord of hosts, and despised the word of the Holy* ***One*** *of Israel.*

Isaiah 10:20 *...the remnant of Israel...shall stay upon the Lord, the Holy* ***One*** *of Israel, in truth.*

Isaiah 29:19 *...the poor among men shall rejoice in the Holy* ***One*** *of Israel.*

Isaiah 30:15 *For thus saith the Lord God, the Holy* ***One*** *of Israel; In returning and rest shall ye be saved...*

Isaiah 30:29 *Ye shall have a song...to the mighty* ***One*** *of Israel.*

Isaiah 31:1 *...they look not unto the Holy* ***One*** *of Israel, neither seek the Lord!*

Isaiah 41:14 *...I will help thee, saith the Lord, and thy redeemer, the Holy* ***One*** *of Israel.*

Isaiah 41:16 *...thou shalt rejoice in the Lord, {and} shalt glory in the Holy* ***One*** *of Israel.*

Isaiah 41:20 *...the Holy* ***One*** *of Israel hath created it.*

Isaiah 43:3 *For I {am} the Lord thy God, the Holy* ***One*** *of Israel, thy Saviour...*

Isaiah 43:14 *Thus saith the Lord, your redeemer, the Holy* ***One*** *of Israel; For your sake I have sent to Babylon...*

Isaiah 43:15 *I {am} the Lord, your Holy* ***One****, the creator of Israel, your King.*

Isaiah 45:11 *Thus saith the Lord, the Holy* ***One*** *of Israel, and his Maker, Ask me of things to come concerning my sons, and concerning the work of my hands command ye me.*

Isaiah 47:4 *{As for} our redeemer, the Lord of hosts {is} his name, the Holy* ***One*** *of Israel.*

Isaiah 48:17 *Thus saith the Lord, thy Redeemer, the Holy* ***One*** *of Israel; I {am} the Lord thy God which teacheth thee to profit, which leadeth thee by the way {that} thou shouldest go.*

Isaiah 49:26 *...all flesh shall know that I the Lord {am} thy Saviour and thy Redeemer, the mighty* ***One*** *of Jacob.*

Isaiah 60:9 *...unto the name of the Lord thy God, and to the Holy* ***One*** *of Israel, because he hath glorified thee.*

Isaiah 60:14 *...they shall call thee; The city of the Lord, The Zion of the Holy* ***One*** *of Israel.*

Isaiah 60:16 *...thou shalt know that I the Lord {am} thy Saviour and thy Redeemer, the mighty* ***One*** *of Jacob.*

Jeremiah 50:29 *...for she hath been proud against the Lord, against the Holy* ***One*** *of Israel.*

Jeremiah 51:5 *...their land was filled with sin against the Holy* ***One*** *of Israel.*

Ezekiel 39:7 *...the heathen shall know that I {am} the Lord, the Holy* ***One*** *in Israel.*

Habakkuk 1:12 *{Art} thou not from everlasting, O Lord my God, mine Holy* ***One****?*

Zechariah 14:9 *And the Lord shall be king over all the earth: in that day shall there be* ***one*** *Lord, and his name* ***one****.*